The American Revolution: A Continuing Commitment

Library of Congress
Symposia on the American Revolution

The American Revolution
A Continuing Commitment

Papers presented at the fifth symposium, May 6 and 7, 1976

Library of Congress   Washington   1976

Library of Congress Cataloging in Publication Data

Library of Congress Symposia on the American
    Revolution, 5th, 1976.
    The American Revolution: A continuing commitment.

    1. United States—History—Revolution, 1775–1783—
Congresses. I. United States. Library of Congress. II. Title.
E204.L53 1976   973.3   76-608237
ISBN 0-8444-0196-X

Advisory Committee

on the Library of Congress

American Revolution Bicentennial Program

John R. Alden
James B. Duke Professor of History Emeritus, Duke University

Julian P. Boyd
Editor of The Papers of Thomas Jefferson, *Princeton University*

Lyman H. Butterfield
Editor in Chief Emeritus of The Adams Papers, *Massachusetts Historical Society*

Jack P. Greene
Professor of History, The Johns Hopkins University

Merrill Jensen
Vilas Research Professor of History, University of Wisconsin

Cecelia M. Kenyon
Charles N. Clark Professor of Government, Smith College

Aubrey C. Land
Research Professor of History, University of Georgia

Edmund S. Morgan
Sterling Professor of History, Yale University

Richard B. Morris
Gouverneur Morris Professor of History Emeritus, Columbia University

George C. Rogers, Jr.
Yates Snowden Professor of American History, University of South Carolina

Introduction

This series of symposia, planned and organized by the American Revolution Bicentennial Office under my general direction and with the cooperation of the Library's advisory committee of distinguished historians of the Revolutionary period, has been made possible by a generous grant from The Morris and Gwendolyn Cafritz Foundation of Washington. The grant also supports the publication of the papers presented at each symposium. The volumes for the four previous symposia have been published under the titles *The Development of a Revolutionary Mentality*, *Fundamental Testaments of the American Revolution*, *Leadership in the American Revolution*, and *The Impact of the American Revolution Abroad*.

This fifth symposium, planned for 1976 as the concluding one of the series, does not deal directly with the history of the Revolution but is rather in the nature of a stocktaking. What has the Revolution meant to America? Have we achieved our dreams or fallen short of them? What new problems face us as we—still a young nation in many ways but a world leader with heavy responsibilities—observe our Bicentennial and contemplate the beginning of our Tricentennial. Thus, in this symposium, we have not turned so much to historians as to authorities in other fields to give us their thoughts and guidance.

Although this symposium is a summing up, I am happy to announce that the Cafritz Foundation, in line with the Library's position that Independence was only *declared* in 1776 and that it took years to win it, has given the Library a grant for another symposium—this one to be held in 1978 and to mark the French Alliance. We are very grateful for this continued support from the foundation.

Presiding over our current symposium will be a distinguished historian and university administrator, David A. Shannon. Vice President and Provost and Commonwealth Professor of History at the University of Virginia, Dr. Shannon received the B.A. degree from Indiana State College and the Ph.M.

and Ph.D. degrees in history from the University of Wisconsin. He held a number of teaching positions—at the Carnegie Institute of Technology, Columbia University, the University of Wisconsin, the University of Maryland, and Rutgers University—before going to the University of Virginia in 1969 as professor of history and dean of the Faculty of Arts and Sciences. He now holds that multititled position which, he says, might be described as vice president for academic affairs. A specialist in recent American history, he has published a number of studies in his field, including *Twentieth Century America: The United States Since the 1890's*, now in its third edition.

It is my pleasure to present Dr. Shannon, who will preside at all the sessions of this two-day symposium.

Elizabeth Hamer Kegan
Assistant Librarian of Congress

Opening Remarks

DAVID A. SHANNON

It is my function to introduce the speakers at this symposium, but before getting to that I have another, very pleasant, task to perform. The Advisory Committee on the Library of Congress American Revolution Bicentennial Program has asked me to read a resolution adopted unanimously by that committee at its meeting on May 6, 1976:

Resolution

Over the past few years the members of the Advisory Committee on the Bicentennial Program of the Library of Congress have watched with growing admiration the extraordinary achievements of the Bicentennial Office under the direction of Elizabeth Hamer Kegan. Because of her foresight, her imagination, and her administrative skill, the Library of Congress has been able to mark the Bicentennial with a rich variety of programs designed to advance understanding of the American Revolution among scholars, among students, and among the public at large. The series of symposia, the reading lists, the bibliographical guides, the reproductions and catalogs of graphic materials, and the great new edition of letters of members of the Continental Congress are Bicentennial achievements of enduring significance, unmatched elsewhere in the nation.

Be it therefore resolved that this committee, being desirous of expressing its gratitude to Mrs. Kegan for this enduring contribution to the national interest, hereby adopts this testimonial of appreciation and requests that copies of its resolution be sent to the Librarian of Congress and to the members of the Joint Committee on the Library.

Contents

The American Revolution: A Continuing Commitment

Professor Paul A. Freund is one of the most eminent legal teacher-scholars in the United States. He has the distinction of having held three different chairs at Harvard. After serving as a professor of law from 1940 to 1950, he became Fairchild Professor of Law for seven years and then Royal Professor of Law for a year before becoming Carl M. Loeb University Professor in 1958, which position he still holds. University professorships at Harvard, according to a university catalog, exist "for men working on the frontiers of knowledge, and in such a way as to cross the conventional boundaries of the specialities." They were designed to free faculty members from affiliation with a department or school and give them a chance to discover the constituencies for teaching that they prefer. Professor Freund regularly teaches a general education course for undergraduates in Harvard College.

Paul Freund graduated from Washington University in 1928 and then studied law at Harvard, taking the L.L.B. in 1931 and the S.J.D. in 1932. He clerked for Mr. Justice Brandeis in 1932–33 and then went into the Roosevelt administration, first with the Department of the Treasury and the Reconstruction Finance Corporation before going to work in the Solicitor General's Office, where he was from 1935 to 1939 and again from 1942 to 1946.

The breadth of his learning and interests are revealed by listing some of the things he has done and been. The list ranges across quite a spectrum of academic and public fields: Vice-president of the Massachusetts Historical Society, a fellow at the Center for Advanced Study in Behavioral Sciences, president of the American Academy of Arts and Sciences, Pitt Professor of American History and Institutions at Cambridge University, 1957–58—and I'm impressed that this was the year he turned 50—and then a little over a year ago, Jefferson Lecturer in the Humanities, the series sponsored by the National Endowment for the Humanities. He has written many law review articles and produced important books, among them On Law and Justice *(1968) and* Cases on Constitutional Law, *first published in 1952. He is editor-in-chief of a monumental work still in preparation,* A History of the Supreme Court.

Liberty and Law
in America

PAUL A. FREUND

"Those who won our independence believed that the final end of the State was to make men free to develop their faculties; and that in its government the deliberative forces should prevail over the arbitrary. They valued liberty both as an end and as a means. They believed liberty to be the secret of happi-ness and courage to be the secret of liberty."

These are the words of Justice Brandeis in the case of *Whitney* v. *California*, decided in 1927, though the last sentence is taken straight from the funeral oration of Pericles as reported by Thucydides. From the Declaration of Inde-pendence onward, "liberty" has indeed been central to the American creed. But what is this liberty, and whose? The liberty of the pike, the saying goes, is the death of the minnows.

Liberty, like life, is a dome of many-colored glass, whose facets need to be looked at one by one. Four of those facets have been a radiant part of our constitutional ideal: liberty of the mind, or freedom of speech, press, and assembly; liberty of the spirit, or the free exercise of religion; liberty of polit-ical participation, or the right of suffrage; and liberty of vocation, or economic freedom. It is to these four liberties that I shall address myself, looking at the ideal and the reality.

"Congress shall make no law . . . abridging the freedom of speech, or of the press." The words of the First Amendment are seemingly absolute. But what exactly is meant by the freedom of speech or of the press? Historically viewed, the guarantee was directed against prior censorship and against the rigors of the English law of seditious libel, which gave the jury only a limited role in criminal prosecutions and which denied the defense of truth, for to the minds of the 18th-century Tory, "the greater the truth the greater the libel." Jefferson himself was no absolutist on freedom of the press. He repeatedly pointed out that private civil suits for damages, brought by a victim of political libel, could be maintained under the laws of the states. Jefferson had no illusions about the excesses of liberty of expression. Writing to a young correspondent in 1807, not too long before he retired from the presidency, he said: "Nothing can now be believed which is seen in a newspaper. Truth itself becomes suspicious by being put into that polluted vehicle." He recommended that a newspaper be divided into four sections, to be entitled Truths, Probabilities, Possibilities, and Lies. The first section, he went on, would be very short. Governmental intervention, however, he steadfastly resisted, as he had in attacking the Sedition Act of 1798 and, as President, in pardoning those convicted under it.

The irrepressible issue of slavery put freedom of the press to a severe test. Congress in 1835 considered and rejected a bill introduced by John C. Calhoun which would have prohibited the delivery in the mail of any material relating to slavery where the receipt of such matter was prohibited by the law of the state of destination. And so the national government not only tolerated but facilitated the distribution of sharply controversial literature. Nevertheless, southern states legislated to require that postmasters notify justices of the peace of the receipt of "incendiary" publications. Suspect materials were to be judged and, if found to be incendiary, burned. Private vengeance was taken against abolitionist literature, reaching its tragic climax in 1837 with the murder of Elijah Lovejoy, editor of the Alton, Illinois, *Observer*, a religious newspaper, while he was protecting his printing press from a proslavery mob. Of this event John Quincy Adams said, "His death gave a shock as of an earthquake throughout this continent, which will be felt in the most distant region of the earth."

War, the threat of war, and the repressive aftermath of war, have created the severest challenges to what Justice Holmes called "freedom for the thought we hate." With some conspicuous and lamentable exceptions, we have been faithful to the Jeffersonian ideal, as can be gathered from that too-little-known volume *Dissent in Three American Wars*, by Samuel Eliot Morison, Frederick Merk, and Frank Freidel, dealing with the wars of the 19th century. The record of the 20th century has been spottier. In the First World War fear was translated into anger, and anger into the proceedings against the socialist journal *The Masses* and into the 20-year sentences meted out to garment workers who had printed and tossed out of a loft window pamphlets denouncing our sending of troops into Russia. In the Vietnam War frustration was translated into anger, and anger into the ill-conceived prosecution of the publicists Benjamin Spock and William Sloane Coffin, Jr.

Recent developments in constitutional law, if they can withstand the pressures of future crises, will make it more difficult to stifle discomforting words. Advocacy of the most radical kind is now deemed immune from criminal prosecution unless and until it becomes actual incitement to violence or to illegal conduct. Prior restraint by injunction, as the Pentagon Papers decision has made clear, is unacceptable, save perhaps in that narrowly defined class of cases where publication would threaten security in a demonstrable and imminent way.

Indeed, in the area of political diatribe and dissemination of news we have moved beyond Jefferson's ideal: while private suits for defamation are allowable under state law, the Fourteenth Amendment, absorbing the First, has been held to require for liability an extremely high showing of culpability on the part of the publisher—actual knowledge of the falsity of the statements or a reckless disregard of their truth or falsity—when the victim who is suing is a public official or a public figure. And outside the field of defamation, in the area of literary or artistic expression (sometimes a euphemism for trash), the law is moving, in my judgment, responsive to a growing mood of toleration, to the point where prosecutions for obscenity will be limited to distribution to juveniles (in aid of parental control), public displays (on an analogy to public nuisances), and zoning violations.

The negative aspect of the ideal of liberty of the mind has been largely achieved: freedom from governmental constraint. But liberty of the mind—and its corollary, freedom of expression—is vindicated not merely for its own sake, not merely as a distinctively human vocation, but as an instrument for the public good, an instrument for the discovery and dissemination of truth. This affirmative aspect requires positive provision, material and intellectual. Liberty to publish is a hollow right indeed if there is no available outlet for one's expression, and it is an empty right if there is no significant content within the mind that seeks expression. These problems of access to the media and quality of publications are more vital issues today than the formal right to speak one's mind.

Technology has given us the mass media, which rarely leave our eyes and ears unassailed. But technology has not made it easier for the individual to put his message into the public domain. On the contrary, the simple days of pamphleteering and the small hand press have gone the way of cottage industry. Access to the media is easy for us as consumers but formidable for us as producers. There is, to be sure, the limited requirement in the field of television that controversial issues be presented fairly—the so-called fairness doctrine, a legal rule which rests on the physically limited number of channels available to a listener, at least in the most commonly used band of frequencies. In the newspaper field the limitation of outlets is also real, but here it is an economic, not a physical, constraint. Should an equivalent fairness doctrine be imposed by law, or at least a right of reply for any person whose character or record has been impugned by a newspaper? Our Supreme Court has rejected such an attempt on the part of a state, in the name of freedom of the press. It was doubtless seen as a dangerous entering wedge by government into the independence of the printed media, though how it was to be distinguished legally from the rule imposed on television was not discussed by the Court. There is, of course, an atmospheric difference: licensing of stations is a practical necessity; licensing of newspapers would be a recrudescence of the treatment of the press by the Stuarts and Tudors. Moreover, the impact of television is uniquely powerful. Finally, in the field of the printed media, although the number of daily papers has shrunk drastically, there are other and perhaps offsetting outlets: weekly news magazines, neighborhood papers, church and trade and labor journals, and the now not-so-underground press. The problem of access nevertheless remains. It becomes a matter of the responsibility of the press itself, to be met by professional self-discipline, whether through the use of an ombudsman, or the letters column, or an overseeing press council.

On the side of content, or access *by* the media, the Freedom of Information Act constitutes a remarkable development in governmental cooperation. Once more the issue becomes responsibility and quality rather than liberty and independence. "If you would bring back the wealth of the Indies, you must carry the wealth of the Indies with you."

When we turn from freedom of the mind and expression to religious freedom we find much the same development. In its American beginnings religious liberty was a somewhat limited ideal. Like so much else in American history it was a function of geographic spaciousness and movement. The Anglican church was established in Virginia and other southern states. The Congregational establishment in Massachusetts not only banished Anne Hutchinson and Roger Williams but excluded Jesuits and Quakers from its shores (with a generous exception in case of shipwreck). The tolerant regimes of Lord Calvert in Maryland, Roger Williams in Rhode Island, and William Penn in Pennsylvania were notable because they were not typical. At the time of the Constitutional Convention only Rhode Island and Virginia enjoyed full religious freedom.

It is all the more remarkable, therefore, that the federal Constitution included a prohibition of all religious tests for national office and, in the First Amendment, a guarantee both of the free exercise of religion and of the nonestablishment of religion. How is this advanced spirit of toleration to be explained? There were undoubtedly a number of causes. In the Revolution our indispensable ally was Catholic France. The influential example of Virginia was powerful. The convention itself was held in the home of Quakerism. A multiplicity of sects was developing, and as Madison believed a multiplicity of economic interests to be a safeguard against the tyranny of a majority, so a multiplicity of sects would be a protection against domination, on a national scale, by a creedal group. Moreover, there were reasons of expediency appropriate to the rise of commercial interests. As the Lords of Trade in London had put it in 1750, toleration and mutual respect were important "to the enriching and improving of a trading nation." The combination of God and Mammon makes an irresistible force.

The free exercise of religion and nonestablishment of religion—you can put the guarantees in a nutshell, but can you keep them there? One's free exercise of religion reaches its limits when it runs against another's free exercise or when it threatens the carrying out of a legitimate secular public purpose. Each of the major religions has had to learn this lesson. Protestants have been particularly aggrieved by the constitutional barrier to prayers and Bible-reading in the public schools (though I know of no barrier to a period of silent meditation). Catholics felt aggrieved when no immunity from military service was allowed for selective conscientious objection to a particular war, based on the Thomistic belief in the doctrine of just and unjust wars. Orthodox Jews who refrained from work on Saturdays felt aggrieved when they were denied an exemption from Sunday closing laws.

As in the case of liberty of speech and press, we have to ask what religious liberty has contributed in an affirmative way to the general good. Ecumenicism has greatly strengthened our sense of community, of unity with respect for diversity. The presidential election of 1960 effectively ended, or so it seems, the element of religious bigotry in national politics that so disfigured the election of 1928. John F. Kennedy was able to defuse the issue as Al Smith had been unable to do. On a minor personal note, I was asked by Senator Kennedy to suggest ways of lightening the issue. I responded by repeating the story told of the late Cardinal Gibbons of Baltimore, who was asked by a lady whether he really believed the pope was infallible. "I can only say, madam," he answered, "that the last time I was in Rome His Holiness called me Cardinal Jibbons." Senator Kennedy used the essence of the story, but for his New York audience the names were changed to Cardinal Spellman and Spillman.

The great, conspicuous failure of religious freedom has been its inability to extirpate racial bigotry, mindless violence, and soulless hatred. Again the uneasy question arises: Liberty, but liberty for what?

Political liberty, or the right of participation in the political process, was left in 1787 to be determined on a state-by-state basis, even with respect to the suffrage for the popularly elected national House of Representatives. This was actually a liberal decision in a twofold sense. For the first time in a federation, one branch of the national legislature was to be elected by the people, not by the states; and if the qualifications for voting had been fixed in the Constitution we would have frozen the standards of the time, which typically confined the suffrage to free males over 21, of civil disposition, who owned 10 pounds' worth of real property or 20 shillings of personal property. With the coming of Jacksonian democracy and the liberalization of the suffrage in the states, this was automatically made applicable to voting for members of Congress. But universal suffrage, which Macaulay predicted would bring the end of civilization, was long in coming. The emancipation of blacks and their enfranchisement after the Civil War too often involved sounding the word of promise to the ear and breaking it to the hope. And women had to wait until living memory to escape from the old common law maxim that husband and wife are one, and he is that one.

Universal suffrage has been achieved, and if in practice it begins to resemble universal apathy the result is not indifference to political liberty. Rather it is a realization that even though we vote directly for our major officeholders we still operate as an indirect democracy, for by and large we vote on candidates, not on specific issues. The system is calculated to produce moderation and accommodation in the legislative process, since there is no either-or decision registered by the electorate. Ours is an electoral, not a plebiscitary, democracy. It was founded at a time when political parties were nonexistent, were suspect and feared. Madison sought to avoid what Ibsen was later to call, in *An Enemy of the People*, a compact majority. Madison envisaged shifting coalitions of diverse interests forming different majorities on different issues. With the early rise of the party system, the constitutional plan might have suffered obliteration. But by a saving irony, the major parties have themselves been coalitions of interests, and this fact, together with the looseness of party discipline, has perpetuated the Madisonian vision long after its historical premise disappeared. Our lawmaking process is fated to be a tedious, often painful process, to the end that the product may be the more broadly acceptable and viable. Political issues, like most of life, are too complex to yield to a binary analysis.

Nevertheless, the sentiment of the people on a given issue and the intensity of feeling it provokes are indispensable ingredients for the decisionmaking process. Political liberty involves some form of access to the process of policymaking at the stage of issues no less than at the stage of candidates for office. Here again the formal liberty of participation derives its vitality from the power and reality of access. Hence the troublesome but understandable phenomenon of taking to the streets as well as to the ballot box. Picketing is the poor person's newspaper, and demonstrations are the lobbying of the lowly. The danger is that the registration of moral and political strength can escalate into intimidation and rule by terror. It has been said that between the First and Second World Wars Germany learned that the allies would never listen to reason but would always yield to force. That lesson led to the degradation and ultimate death of political liberty.

A recurring theme in these remarks has been the importance of material opportunity, not simply formal freedom, in assessing liberty in America. The point becomes cardinal when we view economic liberty.

Thoroughgoing advocates of individual liberty are likely to argue for a minimal state, one whose functions are limited to keeping the peace against violence, punishing fraud, and enforcing agreements. What they overlook is the problem of domination which arises in a polity based on laissez-faire. Does dominance ever become undue, and if so, when? It was questions of this sort that were ignored in that high-water mark of laissez-faire in the Supreme Court, the decision in *Lochner* v. *New York* in 1905 holding that laws limiting the hours of labor in bakeries to 10 hours a day and 60 hours a week were "mere meddlesome interferences with the rights of the individual." It is worth recalling some well-known passages in the majority opinion:

There is no reasonable ground for interfering with the liberty of person or the right of free contract, by determining the hours of labor, in the occupation of a baker. There is no contention that bakers as a class are not equal in intelligence and capacity to men in other trades or manual occupations, or that they are not able to assert their rights and care for themselves without the protecting arm of the State, interfering with their independence of judgment and of action. They are in no sense wards of the State . . . . It is a question of which of two powers or rights shall prevail—the power of the State to legislate or the right of the individual to liberty of person and freedom of contract.

Mr. Justice Peckham had forgotten the parable of the pike and the minnow, and he lived too early to be familiar with the citation at Harvard commencements for the degree in law: "You are prepared to administer those wise restraints that make men free." Free they are, not only because others are restrained, but because in some degree we enhance our own freedom by our fetters. If we were gods, with unlimited freedom to choose and act, we would be more bewildered than free; and who can say that bakers, prevented from binding themselves to 12 hours of labor a day, were the less free as human beings, quite apart from the issue of relief from domination by others?

In the age-old contest between laissez-faire and paternalism, the most important point to remember is not to toot one horn of a dilemma. The problem is one of the mix, and how one resolves that problem will turn on one's temperament and one's judgment of trends. In looking at the proverbial water pitcher, if you are an optimist and reasonably content with the course of things you will say, "It's still half full." If you are assailed by divine discontent you will say, "It's already half empty."

How stands the beaker of liberty? The pursuit of liberty can bring oppression and inhumanity unless it is tempered with equality and fraternity. The pursuit of equality can bring oppression and a deadening of the faculties unless it is tempered with respect for spontaneity, excellence, and enterprise. For a long period of American history liberty took precedence over other values. Now the compensating movement is toward equality. There is no final solution; it is a process of accommodation as endless as the life of a society. Our tradition of liberty is so strong, however, that we are not likely to allow the quest for equality to stamp out the values of excellence and enterprise. We are moving toward equality in basic entitlements, that is, in political participation, in access to the judicial system, in fair procedures for the settlement of conflicts, and, on the ancient principle that a necessitous man is not a free man, in minimum material provision.

In the end the vital solvent is fraternity, which comprehends liberty and equality in a basic respect for individuals, their commonness and their uniqueness. This is essentially a spiritual expression, the manifestation of a fundamental humility. Thomas Hobbes said that we are all equal in our vulnerability while asleep. The ancient Stoics came nearer the mark when they taught that no man is so like unto himself as each is like to all. I would particularize and say that we are all equal in our ignorance of the most basic questions of existence: how did the world come to be, why are we here, whither do we go. In this perspective liberty becomes arrogance unless it is seen as a little candle that each of us holds before his face as he moves amid the inescapable and enveloping shadows of fraternity.

Ambassador Clarence Clyde Ferguson, Jr., has had a varied and distinguished career as attorney, legal educator, and diplomat. After serving four years in the army during World War II, he attended Ohio State University, graduating in 1948. He declined a Rhodes scholarship that year and entered Harvard Law School, where he received the L.L.B. in 1951. He practiced law in New York City and was an assistant United States attorney for the Southern District of New York in 1954 and 1955. He joined the faculty of the Law School of Rutgers University in 1955 and became dean of the Law School at Howard University in 1963, serving in that capacity until 1969. Professor Ferguson has also had a distinguished career in government. From 1961 to 1963 he was general counsel of the United States Commission on Civil Rights. While dean at Howard University, he served as an adviser or member of several United States groups related to the United Nations, and in 1969 he joined the Department of State as special coordinator for relief to the civilian victims of the Nigerian civil war, with the rank of ambassador. He later became an ambassador to Uganda for two years, then deputy assistant secretary of state for African affairs, 1972–73, and then United States representative on the Economic and Social Council of the U.N. He is at present a faculty member of the Law School at Harvard University. Among his publications are Secured Transactions: Article IX, Uniform Commercial Code of New Jersey *(1961),* Desegregation and the Law *(1957), and, with others,* Racism in American Education, *published in 1970.*

Free Men and Revolution
A Black Perspective

CLARENCE CLYDE FERGUSON, JR.

We expect great things from men who have made such a noble stand against the designs of their fellow-men to enslave them.

AGAIN WE CONFRONT the Great American Dilemma. Our subject is not only that pervasive dilemma so uniquely exemplified by its being "American" but also the paradox of our practices and the irony of our professions. Since the appearance of Gunnar Myrdal's *An American Dilemma*[1] in 1942, no American audience needs a dissertation on the nature and dimensions of the horns. There is no more compelling exegesis of that dilemma, the paradox and, ultimately, the irony of our revolutionary profession of two centuries ago, than that of the experience of free black men (and indeed, black women).

The demand for political and personal liberty in the midst of toleration of "that peculiar institution" has quite rightly been described, in the context of colonial Virginia, as an ordeal.[2] A full understanding of the black perspective during the Revolution, by those whose perspectives would be most personal and perhaps most insightful, is difficult to come by. The imperatives of slavery management required the suppression of indigenous African languages, of pagan religions, and of the patterns of loyalties and mutual obligations inherent in the clan—the extended family—and the tribe.[3] Only in the shipboard mutinies, the slave insurrections, and the sermons and spirituals of black slaves do we find the overt expression of a black critique of the nascent American polity.[4] It is in this connection useful to recall that the spiritual "Go Down Moses, Way Down in Egypt Land" was decidedly not a commentary on the condition of the Israelites under the pharaohs. But there were free black men and free black women as well as slaves. Free blacks were a part of the Revolution. They could and did give a black perspective to the American revolt for freedom. Out of that perspective emerges the enduring expression of the Great American Dilemma. And, as with all great dilemmas, it remains unresolved.

Art does not imitate life—art is life. So often the artists among us first perceive and describe our reality and the nature of our being. Thus, in stanzas of two poems by Phillis Wheatley, the black revolutionary perspective manifested itself. Like Jupiter Hammon, a New York slave whose first poem, "Salvation by Christ," appeared in 1760, Wheatley's metaphoric language was that of the Christian religion. The fact that her first poem, written at the age of 14, was a eulogy to Harvard University hardly disturbs this conclusion. On the eve of the Revolution, Phillis Wheatley exclaimed:

> 'Twas mercy brought me from my *Pagan* land,
> Taught my benighted soul to understand
> That there's a God, that there's a *Saviour* too:
> Once I redemption neither sought nor knew.

In the late summer of 1772, Phillis Wheatley completed her statement of the American dilemma in lines to the earl of Dartmouth:

> Should you, my lord, while you peruse my song,
> Wonder from whence my love of *Freedom* sprung,
> Whence flow these wishes for the common good,
> By feeling hearts alone best understood,
> I, young in life, by seeming cruel fate
> Was snatch'd from *Afric's* fancy'd happy seat:
> What pangs excruciating must molest,
> What sorrows labour in my parent's breast?
> Steel'd was that soul and by no misery mov'd
> That from a father seiz'd his babe belov'd:
> Such, such my case. And can I then but pray
> Others may never feel tyrannic sway? [5]

Why, after her first cry, which comes very close to asserting, "Thank God for slavery," this new perspective: "Such, such my case. and can I then but pray/Others may never feel tyrannic sway"? Is this the prayer of an American on the eve of revolution or the plea of a unique new being—the black American?

Phillis Wheatley grasped the essence of the revolutionary paradox for blacks of the Revolution—neither African nor American, being of America but not American, being of Africa but not African. Almost two centuries after the Revolution, the quest for resolution of the paradox continued in the opening lines of Claude McKay's "America":

> Although she feeds me bread of bitterness,
> And sinks into my throat her tiger's tooth,
> Stealing my breath of life, I will confess
> I love this cultured hell that tests my youth!

At once the justification for bondage and hope for salvation *and* freedom, Christianity was undoubtedly the most pervasive force shaping the new species of American—the black American. It was in religion that blacks first organized to confront racism, the great stain on the American character.

In Revolutionary Boston and in Revolutionary Philadelphia, conversion to and practice of the Christian religion by blacks—free and slave—was not so much required as it was assumed. Wheatley's lines marking the passing of just about every Boston minister mark also her close and intimate association with the church. Through her we know that common worship was de rigueur, so much so that there appears to be nothing of note in whites and blacks participating as full communicants in the many services of the church. Indeed, only by happenstance are we made aware that most of Richard Allen's congregations in Radnor, Pennsylvania, were white.[6]

Richard Allen's struggle to resolve this paradox within the metaphor of Christian salvation in a time of revolution adds a dimension which enriches our perspective as did Phillis Wheatley's insightful discovery that she was no longer African.

Allen, a free black itinerant preacher and follower of John Wesley, met the American paradox while on his knees in St. George's Church in Fourth Street, Philadelphia. Born a slave in the household of Benjamin Chew, the chief justice of Pennsylvania during the Revolution, Allen matured in war service in Delaware. During the Revolution he developed a remarkable preaching style which, on his return to Philadelphia "after peace had been declared," was put to service at St. George's at the 5 a.m. meetings. The matter-of-factness of his assignment and his presence at the first conference of Methodist preachers in Baltimore in late 1784 indicate an apparent colorblindness of the church in Revolutionary America. On a fall Sunday morning in 1787, however, Allen and two others were pulled from their knees by white trustees of St. George's. One would like to believe that Richard Allen stood, and in words embedded in thousands of sermons by Allen's successors, proclaimed: "All those who think as I think, follow me." In his own words, hardly less eloquent, he recounted the event:

A number of us usually attended St. George's Church in Fourth Street; and when the colored people began to get numerous in attending the church, they moved us from the seats we usually sat on, and placed us around the wall, and on Sabbath morning we went to church and the sexton stood at the door, and told us to go in the gallery. He told us to go, and we would see where to sit. We expected to take the seats over the ones we formerly occupied below, not knowing any better. We took those seats. Meeting had begun, and they were nearly done singing, and just as we got to the seats, the elder said, "Let us pray." We had not been long upon our knees before I heard considerable scuffling and low talking. I raised my head up and saw one of the trustees, H—— M——, having hold of the Rev. Absalom Jones, pulling him off of his knees, and saying, "You must get up—you must not kneel here." Mr. Jones replied, "Wait until prayer is over." Mr. H—— M—— said, "No, you must get up now, or I will call for aid and force you away." Mr. Jones said, "Wait until prayer is over, and I will get up and trouble you no more." With that he beckoned to one of the other trustees, Mr. L—— S—— to come to his assistance. He came, and went to William White to pull him up.

Allen concluded: "By this time prayer was over and we all went out of the church in a body, and they were no more plagued with us in the church." [7]

A plague? The revolt for freedom had come to this for black Americans. For black Americans what came that Sunday morning in 1787 was the African Methodist Episcopal Church. Why African? The delegates to the Constitutional Convention had already launched the United States of America. A new nation had been forged and Richard Allen and his followers were a part of it. But Allen's church was not the only one to bear the title African. Societies of blacks were being formed in the northern cities and African churches were aborning throughout the states. The choice of *African* offers a clue as to a black retrospective on the meaning of the Revolution to blacks.

In 1773 four slaves in Boston, on behalf of all slaves in the commonwealth, asserted in their petition for freedom:

We expect great things from men who have made such a noble stand against the designs of their *fellow-men* to enslave them. We cannot but wish and hope Sir, that you will have the same grand object, we mean civil and religious liberty, in view in your next session. The divine spirit of *freedom*, seems to fire every humane breast on this continent, except such as are bribed to assist in executing the execrable plan. [8]

There was in the rhetoric of the Revolution a solid basis for expectations of freedom first and then equality. In the *Souls of Black Folk*, William E. B. DuBois wrote:

Before 1750, while the fire of African freedom still burned in the veins of the slaves, there was in all leadership or attempted leadership but the one motive of revolt and revenge,—typified in the terrible Marrons, the Danish blacks, and Cato of Stono, and veiling all the Americas in fear of insurrection. The liberalizing tendencies of the latter half of the eighteenth century brought, along with kindlier relations between black and white, thoughts of ultimate adjustment and assimilation. Such aspiration was especially voiced in the earnest songs of Phyllis, in the martyrdom of Attucks, the fighting of Salem and Poor, the intellectual accomplishments of Banneker and Derham, and the political demands of the Cuffes.[9]

Expectations of great things were, however, disappointed even in the midst of revolution.

But the "souls of black folk" had brought forth something new in the new world:

The Afro-American slaves of the United States, in contradistinction to those in Brazil, Cuba, or Saint-Domingue, inherited Protestant Christianity. Even this diluted and perverted Protestantism lent itself, in various subtle but discernible ways, to the creation of a proto-national black consciousness.[10]

Did we hear in Wheatley and in Allen the cry of *a* new American? Or did we hear in their words the creed of *the* new American?

Upon attaining the Centennial, America celebrated the founding fathers as demigods, or at least as men whose cast was larger than life. Not until the advent of Beard [11] did we begin to tell the truth to ourselves. The founding fathers were human, and while they shaped the course of affairs, they were themselves shaped by the dynamics of their times. It is in the interstices of the freedom-and-slavery paradox that we find the sickening evidence of American racism which would deny revolutionary freedom even to free blacks.

Three-quarters of a century after the American Revolution, Gobineau, described as the "father of racism," [12] observed:

The curious point is that the theory of equality, which is held by the majority of men and so has permeated our customs and institutions, has not been powerful enough to overthrow the evidence against it; and those who are most convinced of its truth pay homage every day to its opposite.[13]

There could be no more apt summary of the problem of the Revolution for Blacks. Racism raises a much more profound issue about the meaning of the American Revolution than even the issue of slavery in the midst of freedom. For the existence of racism must of necessity yield a distorted conception of equality as well as of freedom.

At the moment of revolution slavery existed in every one of the 13 colonies. But there were free black men also in the colonies. In the experience of these free black men we might find a unique perspective from which to judge the meaning of the American Revolution.

The opening rounds of revolt found blacks as fully engaged at Lexington and at Concord as had been Crispus Attucks in the Boston Massacre. That there would have been blacks involved in these opening skirmishes should not be—though it sometimes is—surprising. The presence of some half-million blacks in the colonies of necessity bespoke involvement. And black minutemen were a notable presence on the occasion of the firing of the shot heard round the world.

Captain John Parker's company engaged the British regulars the entire day of April 19, 1775. In the "Bloody Butchery" broadside printed to commemorate the battle of Concord there is listed among the wounded a "Prince Easterbrooks (a Negro Man)." [14] So, too, have we learned of other Black minutemen—Pompy of Braintree, Cato Stedman and Cato Boardman from Cambridge, Cuff Whitemore of Arlington. There were slaves too. Among the Massachusetts companies there was Joshua Boylston's man Prince. John Trumbull's painting of the Battle of Bunker Hill depicts the hero of that day— Peter Salem—as he grasped a musket that is still preserved in the monument in Charlestown, Boston.

Most notable in these early military engagements in Massachusetts was the absence of segregation. Not until the Battle of the Bulge in 1944 would the armed forces of this new nation again witness such a condition. But before the new nation (and its armed forces) could embark upon the experiment in dualism, it had to resolve the issue of whether there was to be black military service at all.

Among the very first general orders issued by George Washington after he assumed command of the Continental army in July 1775 was a directive barring the recruiting of vagabonds and Negroes. The true meaning of this order can be grasped when one recalls that Washington brought his own slave, William Lee, to Cambridge as his body aide and groom, a status Lee kept throughout the Revolutionary War. To fight to make the Revolution a reality was a privilege to be reserved to white men. The mark of racism is thus present at the very creation. We anticipate its recurrence like a defective gene, with a regularity approaching that of Mendel's laws.

It was Prince Hall of Boston who organized a party of blacks to call upon Washington and his adjutant to urge that blacks be permitted to volunteer for service in the army of the colonies. There followed almost six months of debate in Washington's command and in Congress. In October Washington and his general officers concluded that the army had to remain white. And on November 12, 1775, Washington issued an order barring all blacks—free and slave alike—from the Continental line. The issue then was not status, free or slave. The issue was race—whether one's color was black or white. Only the necessities apparent at Valley Forge and the less than sterling performance of the sunshine patriots combined to compel a reversal of Washington's dictate. Thus when we now examine the dramatic painting of Washington crossing the Delaware, sharp eyes detect a black American wielding the stroke oar—Prince Whipple of New Hampshire.

But it was also Prince Hall who approached, successfully, a British regiment to obtain a provisional charter for a lodge of black Freemasons. And it is in these two actions of Prince Hall, dealing equally with revolutionists and the established English authority, that we gain a true black perspective on the Revolution.

Probably some five thousand blacks served the Revolutionary cause under arms. More than likely an equal number served the cause of the king. There is, however, no inconsistency in this duality. Blacks fought for the side perceived to be most responsive to the peculiar needs of blacks. Their interests were not coterminous with the interests of their white Revolutionary compatriots—neither were they identical with those of the Loyalists. Service in the Revolutionary cause brought freedom for an unknown number of blacks. Similarly, service in the king's cause was rewarded. Some fourteen thousand blacks evacuated by the British from New York, Charleston, and Savannah began a new journey to freedom—for some to the West Indies and for others home again to West Africa. Moreover, as many as a hundred thousand blacks "voted with their feet"—to the swamps, over the mountains to the West, and in with Indian tribes.[15]

What kinds of services were rendered by blacks in the Revolution?

The black soldier and sailor of the Revolution, whether he fought for Congress or king, served in a variety of ways—as infantryman, artilleryman, scout, guide, spy, guard, courier, waggoner, orderly, cook, waiter, able seaman, privateersman, and military laborer of all sorts. In a few cases, blacks formed their own units.[16]

Among the blacks forming black Revolutionary units was Colonel Middleton of Boston: the colonel believed the rhetoric of the American Revolution and had fought for its realization.

Revolution's aftermath for black Americans was, however, bitter indeed. Racism was abroad in the land. We have seen that symptoms of racism—not merely the problem of slavery—were present at the very creation. There are, of course, denials that racism was a factor in the Revolution and its aftermath. There is even the suggestion that American racism was an outgrowth of slavery: "In the South, for example, militant race superiority evolved out of the defense of plantation slavery, to become an ingredient in the culture." [17]

It is at least arguable that racism was a special development in American thought which, while obviously closely related to slavery justifications, none-theless had developed independently of the slave system.

By two decades after Lexington and Concord and Breed's Hill, blacks were fair game on the streets of Boston. In June 1797 Prince Hall charged his African Lodge of Masons on the occasion of their Feast of St. John as follows:

Patience, I say; for were we not possess'd of a great measure of it you could not bear up under the daily insults you meet with in the streets of Boston: much more on public days of recre-ation, how are you shamefully abus'd, and that at such a degree that you may truly be said to carry your lives in your hands, and the arrows of death are flying about your heads.[18]

Lerone Bennett, Jr. Recounts the shattering of the dream of seventy-six:

The arrows of death and humiliation whistled about the head of Colonel Middleton, another Revolutionary War veteran. During a Boston riot, a group of whites attacked Negroes in front of his home. The old soldier stuck a musket out of his door and threatened to kill any white man who approached. One of his neighbors, a white man, asked the whites to leave. Then he approached Colonel Middleton and begged him to put away his gun. Colonel Middle-ton stood silent for a moment. Then he turned and tottered off, dropping his gun and weeping as he went.
Colonel Middleton's America, Prince Hall's America and Thomas Jefferson's America tottered into the nineteenth century, divided and afraid.[19]

Expectations of great things were disappointed.

> What happens to a dream deferred?
>   Does it dry up
>   like a raisin in the sun?
>   Or fester like a sore—
>   And then run?
>   Does it stink like rotten meat?
>   Or crust and sugar over—
>   like a syrupy sweet?
>   Maybe it just sags
>   like a heavy load.
>   Or does it explode? [20]

While the racist roots of Washington's exclusionary order barring military service by blacks—free and slave alike—are apparent, much more attention has been focused on Washington's fellow Virginian Thomas Jefferson. Of course, this focus is not misplaced, for Jefferson is indeed the intellectual embodiment of our Revolutionary precepts. Beyond that, however, Jefferson was also the embodiment of the American paradox. And as befits his in-tellectual stature, Jefferson exhibited the paradox in a most complex and subtle fashion. There is no question that the slave owner Thomas Jefferson was genuinely opposed to slavery.[21] There is also little question but that Jeffer-son was also a racist.

Thomas Jefferson's own commentary on the Continental Congress' failure to outlaw slavery in the southern territories (south of the Ohio River) are token of his antislavery stance. Referring to the proceedings of the Congress on March 16, 1785, he wrote:

... there were 10. states present. 6. voted unanimously for it, 3. against it, and one was divided: and seven votes being requisite to decide the proposition affirmatively, it was lost. The voice of a single individual of the state which was divided, or of one of those which were of the negative, would have prevented this abominable crime from spreading itself over the new country. Thus we see the fate of millions unborn hanging on the tongue of one man, and heaven was silent in that awful moment! [22]

There appears to be a considerable question as to the bona fides of Jefferson's well-known antislavery expressions.[23] Some credence should be lent, however, to the fact of public espousals of restrictions on slavery. Fully two years before the "slavery charge" was striken from the Declaration of Independence, Jefferson had already arraigned the crown for refusing to prohibit the importation of slaves.[24] One need not go so far as to endorse the assertion that "it is just and fitting that every person of African descent who goes into Jefferson's Memorial and reads its inscriptions should take away with him the knowledge that his race is indebted to Thomas Jefferson as the American Statesman who began the fight against African Slavery in the United States" [25] in order to ascribe to Jefferson a position of opposition to the institution of slavery— no matter what his real motivations might have been.

A black perspective on the American Revolution must engage on its own terms not merely slavery but also racism. It is the problem of racism which raises the much more profound Jeffersonian question. The profundity lies in the fact that there appears to be evidence that Jefferson's racism was characteristic of the American Revolutionary mentality and represented an intellectual imperative much beyond the merely deterministic justification of a predominantly southern economic system.

Jefferson's reaction to Phillis Wheatley provides an early clue to the existence of the racist fault:

Among the blacks is misery enough, God knows, but no poetry .... The compositions published under her name are below the dignity of criticism.[26]

But there is much more direct evidence as to Jefferson's conception of race than the inferences which might be drawn from a few lines of literary riposte.

Why not retain and incorporate the blacks into the state, and thus save the expence of supplying by importation of white settlers, the vacancies they will leave? Deep rooted prejudices entertained by the whites; ten thousand recollections, by the blacks, of the injuries they have sustained; new provocations; the real distinctions which nature has made; and many other circumstances, will divide us into parties, and produce convulsions, which will probably never

end but in the extermination of the one or the other race. To these objections, which are
political, may be added others, which are physical and moral. The first difference which strikes
us is that of colour. Whether the black of the negro resides in the reticular membrane between
the skin and the scarf-skin [epidermis], or in the scarf-skin itself; whether it proceeds from the
colour of the blood, the colour of the bile, or from that of some other secretion, the difference
is fixed in nature, and is as real as if its seat and cause were better known to us. And is this
difference of no importance? Is it not the foundation of a greater or less share of beauty in the
two races? Are not the fine mixtures of red and white, the expressions of every passion by
greater or less suffusions of colour in the one preferable to that eternal monotony, which reigns
in the countenances, that immoveable veil of black which covers all the emotions of the other
race? Add to these, flowing hair, a more elegant symmetry of form, their own judgment in
favour of the whites, declared by their preference of them, as uniformly as is the preference of
the Oranootan [orangutan] for the black women over those of his own species. The circum-
stance of superior beauty, is thought worthy attention in the propagation of our horses, dogs,
and other domestic animals; why not in that of man? Besides those of colour, figure, and hair,
there are other physical distinctions proving a difference of race. They have less hair on the
face and body. They secrete less by the kidnies, and more by the glands of the skin, which
gives them a very strong and disagreeable odour. This greater degree of transpiration renders
them more tolerant of heat, and less so of cold than the whites. Perhaps too a difference of
structure in the pulmonary apparatus . . . may have disabled them from extricating, in the
act of inspiration, so much of that fluid from the outer air, or obliged them in expiration, to
part with more of it. They seem to require less sleep. A black after hard labour through the
day, will be induced by the slightest amusements to sit up till midnight, or later though knowing he must be out with the first dawn of the morning. They are at least as brave, and more
adventuresome. But this may perhaps proceed from a want of fore-thought, which prevents
their seeing a danger till it be present. When present, they do not go through it with more
coolness or steadiness than the whites. They are more ardent after their female: but love seems
with them to be more an eager desire, than a tender delicate mixture of sentiment and sensation. Their griefs are transient. Those numberless afflictions, which render it doubtful whether
heaven has given life to us in mercy or in wrath, are less felt, and sooner forgotten with them.
In general, their existence appears to participate more of sensation than reflection. To this
must be ascribed their disposition to sleep when abstracted from their diversions, and unemployed in labour. An animal whose body is at rest, and who does not reflect, must be dis-
posed to sleep of course. Comparing them by their faculties of memory, reason, and imagination, it appears to me that in memory they are equal to the whites; in reason much inferior,
as I think one could scarcely be found capable of tracing and comprehending the investigations
of Euclid.[27]

It should be noted at this point that Benjamin Banneker's comprehension of
Euclid, as well as that of L'Enfant, has blessed Washington with its street
pattern. The ultimate expression of racism is encapsulated in Jefferson's
single sentence: "I advance it therefore as a suspicion only, that the blacks
whether originally a distinct race, or made distinct by time and circumstances,
are inferior to the whites in the endowments both of body and mind." [28]

Jefferson's views were not atypical, nor were they the views of the planter
class alone. In Boston, Prince Hall had experienced a decade of frustration in

attempting to procure a full charter for his lodge of African Freemason. Jeremy Belknap, pressed into service to investigate the problem in 1795, exposed the basis of white Masonic resistence to chartering the African Lodge. A leading white Mason informed Belknap that:

The African Lodge, though possessing a charter from England, meet by themselves; and white masons not more skilled in geometry, will not acknowledge them. . . . The truth is, they are *ashamed* of being on *equality* with blacks.[29]

The totality of the black perspective and presence in the time of revolution is not described, however, by the identification of racism as a dominant shaping force of that black presence. The seeds of abolition and, indeed, of anti-racism were already sown before the Revolution.[30] It took nearly a century to come to terms with the institution of slavery by abolishing it, and it has taken nearly a second century to engage the forces of racism in our polity. We are indeed far from the abolition of institutionalized racism in American life. We are, however, on the verge of a national consensus that this evil conception is inconsistent with that which we purport to be and inconsistent with that which we are to become. There can be no more noble contribution to the celebration of the American Bicentennial than the expression of the hope that upon the Tricentennial all Americans can join in the spiritual given to our country by its black compatriots:

> Free at last, Free at last,
> Thank God Almighty, Free at last.

Notes

[1] Gunnar Myrdal, *An American Dilemma: The Negro Problem and Modern Democracy* (New York: Harper & Brothers, 1944).

[2] Edmund S. Morgan, *American Slavery, American Freedom: The Ordeal of Colonial Virginia* (New York: Norton, 1975).

[3] See Herbert Aptheker, *Essays in the History of the American Negro* (New York: International Publishers, 1973), pp. 1–15.

[4] See, for example, Peter H. Wood, *Black Majority: Negroes in Colonial South Carolina from 1670 through the Stono Rebellion* (New York: Knopf, 1974), passim.

[5] Phillis Wheatley, *Poems on Various Subjects, Religious and Moral* (London: A. Bell, 1773), pp. 18 74.

[6] Sidney Kaplan, *The Black Presence in the Era of the American Revolution, 1770–1800* (Greenwich, Conn.: New York Graphic Society, 1973), pp. 171–78.

[7] Ibid., p. 81.

[8] Peter Bestes, et al., "Sir, The Efforts made by the legislative of this province . . .," broadside, April 20, 1773, New-York Historical Society. Photocopy, Boston Public Library.

[9] William E. B. DuBois, *The Souls of Black Folk* (1903), reprinted in *Three Negro Classics* (New York: Avon Books, 1965), p. 244.

[10] Eugene D. Genovese, *Roll, Jordon, Roll: The World the Slaves Made* (New York: Pantheon Books, 1974), p. 168.

[11] Charles Austin Beard, *An Economic Interpretation of the Constitution* (New York: Free Press, 1941).

[12] Michael D. Biddiss, ed., *Gobineau: Selected Political Writings* (New York: Harper & Row, 1970), p. 13.

[13] Ibid., p. 72.

[14] "Bloody butchery, by the British Troops . . . Battle of Concord, April 19, 1775," broadside (Salem, N.E.: E. Russell, 1775), Massachusetts Historical Society, line 9 under "Wounded from Lexington."

[15] Aptheker, *Essays*, pp. 73–110.

[16] Kaplan, *Black Presence*, p. 32.

[17] John Hope Franklin, *The Militant South: 1800–1861* (Cambridge: Belknap Press of Harvard University Press, 1970), p. xi.

[18] Prince Hall, *A Charge Delivered to the African Lodge, June 24, 1797, at Menotomy* [West Cambridge (Boston: Printed by Benjamin Edes, for and sold at Prince Hall's Shop, 1797).

[19] Lerone Bennett, Jr., *Before the Mayflower; a History of the Negro in America, 1619–1966* (Baltimore: Penguin Books, 1973), p. 69.

[20] Langston Hughes, "Dream Deferred," copyright © 1959, 1967 by Langston Hughes. Reprinted from *The Panther and the Lash; Poems of Our Times* (1967) by Langston Hughes, by permission of the publisher, Alfred A. Knopf.

[21] See Winthrop D. Jordon, *White Over Black: American Attitudes toward the Negro, 1550–1812* (Chapel Hill: Published for the Institute of Early American History and Culture at Williamsburg, Va., by the University of North Carolina Press, 1968), pp. 430 *et seq.*

[22] Thomas Jefferson, *The Papers of Thomas Jefferson*, ed. Julian P. Boyd, vol. 10 (Princeton, N.J.: Princeton University Press, 1954), p. 58.

[23] David Brion Davis, *The Problem of Slavery in the Age of Revolution: 1770–1823* (Ithaca, N.Y.: Cornell University Press, 1975), pp. 164–212.

[24] Ibid., p. 173.

[25] Jefferson Randolph Kean, "Thomas Jefferson and African Slavery," in Elbert D. Thomas, *Thomas Jefferson, World Citizen* (New York: Modern Age Books, 1942), p. 265.

[26] Thomas Jefferson, *Jefferson's Notes, on the State of Virginia* (Baltimore: W. Pechin, 1800), p. 144.

[27] Ibid., pp. 141–43.

[28] Ibid., p. 147.

[29] Kaplan, *Black Presence*, p. 191.

[30] Davis, *Problem of Slavery*, pp. 213–84.

Erik Barnouw, professor emeritus of dramatic arts at Columbia University, was born at The Hague; his family moved to this country in 1919. After graduating from Princeton in 1929, he worked as a writer for Fortune *magazine briefly and then spent a year in Europe on a traveling fellowship, during which he studied with Max Reinhardt in Vienna. Upon his return to America he went into broadcasting as a director and writer. In 1946 Professor Barnouw joined the faculty of Columbia University and continued his work in broadcasting, primarily as a writer for the Theatre Guild radio and television series. He also organized the Center for Mass Communication, a unit of the Columbia University Press. He did some outstanding films for this center—for example, a series on constitutional law entitled* Decision, *which he wrote for National Educational Television with the assistance of Herbert Wechsler of the Columbia University School of Law. He also produced the center's film* Hiroshima-Nagasaki, 1945, *which appeared on public television on the 25th anniversary of the Hiroshima bombing and which received several awards.*

Professor Barnouw has written about radio and television as well as for it. His best known work on broadcasting is a three-volume set entitled History of Broadcasting in the United States. *The first volume,* A Tower in Babel, *appeared in 1966 and the next two at two-year intervals,* The Golden Web *in 1968 and* The Image Empire *in 1970. In 1975 he updated the material and condensed these three volumes into a single but still large book entitled* Tube of Plenty: The Evolution of American Television. *This masterful series has received important prizes, among them the Frank Luther Mott Award in the history of journalism and the Bancroft Prize in American history.*

Another of his major contributions is Documentary: A History of Non-fiction Film, *published by the Oxford University Press in 1974, which was based on research in film archives in 20 different nations.*

In 1976 he became a fellow of the Woodrow Wilson International Center for Scholars, Smithsonian Institution.

The Media Revolution

ERIK BARNOUW

IT SEEMS ALTOGETHER APPROPRIATE at a Bicentennial symposium to have a look at the media revolution, for that revolution, as I see it, has been going on throughout much of the 200-year history of our country and may have played a larger role in it than is generally supposed.

And in a discussion of the American Revolution as a continuing phenomenon —involving also, in the words of our symposium subtitle, a continuing commitment—a look at the media revolution is not only appropriate but essential. For nothing seems more certain than that upheavals in our web of communication are not just a phenomenon of the past but will continue into the future, bringing great changes in the years to come. The revolution will go on.

The general nature of the changes—not only those of yesterday and today but those of tomorrow as well—can probably be described without too much difficulty and without too much disagreement. Far more difficult is the problem of discerning their effects on our lives, our mores, our view of the world, our beliefs, our institutions, our actions. Not so long ago, such matters did not arouse much interest, but today they do. Just as we no longer take for granted the air we breathe and the life-support system of our planet, so we no longer take for granted our psychic environment as conditioned by communication media. The possible effects of this environment on crucial aspects of our lives have become matters of wide discussion. Their consideration at this symposium is, I suppose, testimony to that.

Perhaps we should begin with a 200-year backward look. The psychic environment of 1776 was mainly a matter of communication between people.

News of the larger world came mostly by word of mouth—fed, however, by a trickle of printed matter produced for the few who could read. The trickle consisted of newspapers, pamphlets, broadsides, and books. The newspapers were often read aloud in the coffeehouses. They were the main media network of the time.

To call them "newspapers" may be misleading. Most were grimy, four-page newsletters, issued weekly or irregularly. One piece of paper, folded once, was the prevailing format. On the eve of independence there were about three dozen such sheets in the colonies. A paper was likely to be the product of one man, a printer. He printed reader contributions, essays, reports from travelers, and items cribbed from other papers. Subscribers generally numbered in the hundreds rather than in the thousands.

Even if a printer could have sold more copies, he would probably have had a hard time printing them. He had to set all type by hand, and each sheet of paper had to be carefully laid in position by hand. Technically, his procedure was close to that of the Gutenberg era.

Even if he could have printed more copies, he might not have been able to get the paper. Most paper was imported. If newspapers appeared irregularly, it was partly because of a chronic shortage of paper.

None of these newspapers employed anyone we would call a reporter. The idea of going out to look for news had not yet entered American journalism.

These papers carried bits of advertising that tell us a good deal about the period. Many announced the arrival of items from abroad—linens, or ladies' gloves, or other manufactured items. No hard sell was needed. The mere announcement of such a shipment seemed enough to bring customers running, since the colonies, for all their bounteous blessings, faced a number of shortages. If this was the case for linens and ladies' gloves, it also applied to printed words. These too were a scarce item, and that fact helps to explain why the newspapers, so skimpy and unspectacular, were also powerful. Printed words could be precious. They were not just glanced at and cast aside. Often they were read, reread, and read aloud. In that way the papers became a means through which the ferment of the revolution, and later the debates over the Bill of Rights, spread throughout the land. The reader went in search of the word, just as the buyer went in search of the product. It was, an economist would say, a seller's market.[1]

If one wished to summarize in a few words the startling changes in communication over the past 200 years, one might well begin with the transition from a seller's to a buyer's market—in words, in images, and in sounds. Today we have a glut of all of these, as well as of many other things. It used to be said that if you built a better mousetrap, the world would beat a path to your door. That used to have truth in it, but surely it is nonsense today. Every better mousetrap—and every coffeemaker, headache tablet, automobile, stomach settler, pocket calculator, toothpaste, cakemix, paper towel, floorwax, and furniture spray, whether last year's version or this year's new and improved model—pursues you relentlessly. Its image confronts you in your morning paper. It cajoles you from your radio during your ride to work. It shouts at you from billboards and magazines. And at home, in living color—more living, more colorful than anything you saw all day—it faces you from the luminous television screen. It has tracked you to your home, as have the words, sounds, and images of education, of religion, and of politics. The path to your door has been beaten not by the customer but by the mousetrap—and the word.

The presence of all this competitive communication within the home, its frequent domination of the home, its replacement of the hearth as the focus of the home, and its displacement of other influences—including, to some extent, interpersonal relationships—are perhaps the most crucial aspects of the media revolution. But before we examine these, let us consider some other aspects of this revolution.

The colonial press was supported mainly by its subscribers. Advertising was a minor source of income. But soon this began to change. When a young job printer, Benjamin Day, decided in the early 1830's to start a new paper, the New York *Sun*, he resolved to charge just one cent for it instead of the prevailing price of six cents He was applying a formula already proved successful in England.

In America, independence had brought an eruption of factories, which had been discouraged under colonial rule. But their mass production of products could be justified only by sales over a wide geographic area, and this called for widespread product advertising. To attract this burgeoning business, Benjamin Day became a mass producer of words—on paper that was now also mass produced and plentiful. Casting aside his old-style handpress, he imported a steam press and soon found himself able to serve a circulation of 20,000 copies, the largest in the world. He was turning out a paper of many pages, crammed with news *and* advertising, that may have cost 20 cents or more to print and distribute but that the reader could buy for one cent. Mass communication had crossed a fateful Rubicon—it had become largely advertising supported, instead of audience supported. The culmination of that transition is, of course, on the television screen or screens in your home, where drama and news and cultural events are made possible, as the saying goes, by sponsors, advertisers, and underwriters. The competition for this support, and for audiences, has become strenuous and unrelenting. Some media, to be sure, have remained audience supported—books, for example. But the competitive struggle for attention—in other words, for survival—has affected the tone and content even of these.

The change of tone was already evident in the 1830's, when the *Sun* led the explosion of America's penny papers. Those papers were trying to reach a new class of readers—the artisans and mechanics, who with the rise of industry were becoming conscious of themselves as a group. They were beginning to read. Public school education was beginning. Trade unions were forming.

To cater to this group, Benjamin Day sent a fellow printer, at four dollars a week, to attend police court trials and report the lurid details—which he did in a spicy, mocking tone. Thus the reporter entered American journalism. Day also inaugurated vigorous promotion. He sold copies to newsboys at 67 cents a hundred and sent them into the streets to shout the horrifying and dramatic headlines. A decade later news "by telegraph" began to add to the sensational content as well as to the geographic scope. Circulations rose astoundingly.

But not everyone was happy about the new tone. The penny papers were said to be corrupting the young and encouraging crime. A father, protesting to a Boston newspaper, said that he would rather see his children "in their graves while pure in innocence, than dwelling with pleasure upon these reports, which have grown so bold." Horace Greeley, who founded the New York *Tribune* in 1841, condemned the penny papers for being willing, as he put it, to "fan into destroying flames the hellish passions which now slumber in the bosom of society." He said: "The guilt of murder may not stain their hands; but the fouler and more damning guilt of making murderers." The penny papers were not penitent. To expose crime, they kept saying, was to discourage it. Wherever villainy deserved exposure, Benjamin Day had said, he would "lash the rascals naked through the world."

James Gordon Bennett, founder of the *Sun*'s competitor, the New York *Herald*, expressed his sense of mission with even greater enthusiasm—and, one might say, with considerable lack of modesty. He said: "Books have had their day—theaters have had their day—the temple of religion has had its day. A newspaper can be made to take the lead of all these in the great movements of human thought and of human civilization. A newspaper can send more souls to Heaven, and save more from Hell, than all the churches and chapels in New York—besides making money at the same time." Within a few years the *Herald* was the biggest money-maker of the New York newspapers.[2]

One thing we can say about these pronouncements, from our vantage of a later century, is that they sound familiar. The style of rhetoric has changed, not the message. Similar warnings of doom, similar assertions of an evangelical mission, accompanied the rise of the motion picture at the turn of the century, of some of the later mass magazines, of broadcasting in the 1920's, of the comic book, and finally, of television. The young were in each case a focus of concern. The concern came especially from those who had a traditional role in the raising of the young—parent, school, and church. They felt that an old balance of influences was being upset, and they were right. With the rise of television, they have been joined in their concern by others—and again, with some reason. For as television established its hegemony, the earlier media that had once been seen as threats were joining the displaced. Now they too saw their roles diminishing, they too felt the ground slipping under them and sensed a crumbling of the social order.[3]

In view of the rising chorus of concern, we might have a closer look at what television means to its audience, especially the young. For some time the Roper organization has periodically asked people from what source they learn what's going on in the world today—from the newspapers or radio or television or magazines or talking to people or where? Since 1963 the majority of people have said television, and in subsequent years the percentage giving this answer has kept growing. For many, television seems virtually the only source of information about world happenings. The majority also describe television as the "most trusted" medium.

Such findings might be interpreted at first glance as a tribute to television as a news medium, but this conclusion seems unwarranted. Research tends to show that the young, the most rabid viewers, watch almost no news programs until they are halfway through high school, and even then only about half become news-watchers. By that time most have seen at least 20,000 television programs and a picture of the world has taken firm root, without much of a contribution from newscasts. In a sense, other kinds of programming have become the journalism of the young.

Today a child becomes conscious of television at a remarkably early age. Recently a Columbia University student wrote in a term paper that his first television memory was of having his diaper changed by an annoyed mother who was trying to keep her eyes glued to a television screen. He sensed that he had created an inopportune mess but that the tube was a far more important focus for attention. Before long it became that for him too, first through various warm-hearted television uncles, aunts, and strange animals and then—very soon thereafter—through scenes of action.

Since the mid-1950's television schedules have been crammed with so-called action-adventure drama—a genre that at long last seems to be declining in quantity but is still prominent. It concerns cowboys, crime-busters, spies, or other heroes. Essentially, all represent the same formula: Someone must catch or kill an evil person, and does. For the young, these programs seem to present the world beyond the home, and millions have been brought up on them. Research studies such as those of Wilbur Schramm at Stanford University have shown this to be almost the sole television diet of most children during the elementary school years and partway through secondary school. Only in the final high school years do some begin to be aware of another world —seen through print or news programs or public television—while the others stick to the action-adventure world. The two worlds are almost incompatible.[4]

For harassed parents it has been easy to look on all this viewing as entertainment comparable to that which they experienced years earlier at the Saturday afternoon movies. But however similar they may be in content, the two activities are very different in status and function. Saturday at the movies was unlike anything else one did all week and was especially wondrous for that reason. It was surcease from daily routine. Television action-adventure *is* daily routine. It may go on for hours each day. It has become a continual backdrop to home life, a kind of living wallpaper. In some homes it continues through meals, short-circuiting other communication. In many it occupies more hours than anything but sleep. And it emanates from a luminous tube that represents the larger world and carries authority. In living color, more living and more colorful than one's own life, it defines life's possibilities.

Of course, this is a traditional role for story telling. Through stories we have always learned what the world is like, what we are like, and what we might become. But never before have people been surrounded so constantly by living symbols of themselves acting out the good and the bad, the desirable and the undesirable. The machinery of television, with its sponsors, has in a very real sense taken over the acculturation process, displacing grandma, grandpa, school, church, and other media.

Don't underestimate the impact. This "entertainment" has, to begin with, a documentary quality. Some series are proclaimed as being based on the files of this or that police department. You see the actual locations. On some you are told that only names are changed to protect the innocent. At the end of a program in the series entitled *The FBI*, an authoritative voice says that so-and-so was sentenced to six years in the penitentiary—even though the story was invented by a scriptwriter. On some spy series various actual countries are mentioned and famous places are shown. *The Man From U.N.C.L.E.* brought many letters to the United Nations from applicants for jobs at U.N.C.L.E. Signs of authenticity are everywhere.

Of course, all this was not consciously meant to fool people. It was showmanship designed to win an audience and, for sponsors, to sell a product. The audience may itself have considered it entertainment while at the same time accepting it as essentially true. Television drama thus may function informationally or journalistically without being so labeled. The late J. Edgar Hoover certainly thought so, to judge by the dogged attention he gave to liaison with television and comic book producers. His saga seems to tell us that mythology is the road to congressional appropriations.

In the acculturation process, action-adventure programming is of course supplemented by other genres, notably the commercial. If action-adventure drama tells how problems of society are solved, the commercial tells how to solve personal problems: by buying products. It does so in mini-dramas, or in songs that have become the folksongs of our time, endlessly repeated by the young. These—like the shows in which they are embedded—picture a world in which all problems seem to have instant, clearcut solutions, pushbutton or pill-popping solutions. Again, no one intends such a sweeping message. Again, results go beyond intentions.

It is worth looking for a moment at the kind of world that may emerge from this mythology in the minds of the young. It is a world that seldom admits of poverty. Even its murder mysteries take place against backgrounds of the better life. The message is zealously furthered by game and quiz shows, in which almost everyone is showered with luxury items. It is worth recalling that on one quiz series the consolation prize for losers was a Cadillac. Into this extravaganza atmosphere a documentary occasionally injects a sobering, disruptive note so discordant that it is at once condemned as subversive propaganda. The producer of *Hunger in America*, a CBS documentary, found himself being investigated by the FBI.

It is a world that seems to face few problems that cannot be solved by catching or killing some evil person. Other kinds of problems seldom appear on action-adventure drama. The programming would seem to be fertile soil for law-and-order politics.

Other implications are worth a mention. In books, theater, and radio, crime dramas have usually ended with identification and arrest of a lawbreaker. In television it has long been standard procedure for the villain to make a break at the end so that he has to be chased up and down a canyon or fire escape or catwalk, with a final solution through fist, gunfire, karate, dagger, or whatever. The endless repetition of this formula suggests an unspoken premise: that in our world the organized procedures of justice are inadequate, are not to be relied on—that in the end all problems call for the physical action of a hero. It is a message with possible vigilante overtones.

The recent spate of spy dramas involved other implications. Writers for *Mission: Impossible* received written instructions to the effect that the villains, who represented unidentified foreign countries, must be so evil and so clever that the intricate means used to defeat them are necessary. This series and others like it promoted an essentially paranoid view of the world and seemed to provide a continuing rationale for covert action. Even the official lie was part of the formula as originally prescribed on *Mission: Impossible:* "Should you . . . be caught," the secret agents were always told, "the Secretary will disavow any knowledge of your actions." Of course, this was intended as entertainment, not as propaganda. One's own entertainment is not generally seen as propaganda, although other people's is. But through such entertainment, unspoken premises may become a society's axioms.[5]

In relation to the media revolution, I would like to suggest that we have been seeing a fascinating—and thought-provoking—scrambling of genres and functions. We used to think of journalism, entertainment, education, politics, advertising, and religion as somewhat separate activities, each carried on in its own proper domain, with its own procedures. But today the bright tube, in living color, has become the newspaper, theater, schoolroom, podium, billboard, and pulpit. In the process, all have gravitated toward the same dramaturgical techniques and appeals. It is all part of the feverish struggle for the crowning spotlight.

While entertainment is assuming a journalistic function, government is becoming a kind of show business. Major government moves are considered in terms of television impact. When the Kennedy administration was planning its response to the Cuban missile crisis of 1962, the various alternative plans were all referred to as scenarios and each had its proposed television climax. The word *scenario* seems to have become a standard term in government planning. A few years later when the newly elected President, Richard Nixon, introduced his cabinet on television, with all the wives, the ritual seemed to be modeled on the Ed Sullivan program. During the moon flight, the astronauts recited passages from the Book of Genesis as they rounded the moon; not only the reading but also its precise timing had apparently been planned much earlier by NASA. From the surface of the moon, astronaut Armstrong talked to the President on a split television screen, and even the dialogue was scripted. All this caused the television critic for the *Saturday Review*, Robert Lewis Shayon, to wonder whether there would ever again be "pure events"—assuming there ever had been. He predicted: "Everything hereafter will be stage-managed for cosmic Nielsens, in the interest of national and universal establishments."[6] Meanwhile the politician running for the Senate may find himself spending a fortune for a few minutes of television time; then, to make certain they yield maximum impact, he hires writers, directors, and film crews and finds himself producing and starring in mini-documentaries. When an evangelist rents a stadium for a revival meeting, it may be merely the first step in the production of another kind of television spectacular.

Amid all this showmanship, the newsman feels the pressure. In television he has generally presented sequences of information fragments, each without context. Such fragments are incomprehensible to some and offer little scope for emotional identification. That is why he has reached few viewers among the young. To remedy this, station after station hires consultants to augment the show-business appeal of news programs. The remedies seem to affect both form and content: the subject matter of the more popular news shows often echoes that of action-adventure drama. Crime, of course, is a favorite, and the criminal proves a helpful collaborator. He often seems to plan his crime for television: it is his own scenario for a moment in the world's spotlight.

Amid such trends, who can see the borderline between fact and fiction, information and persuasion, education and propaganda, news and entertainment? Is there a dividing line? And when we are asked the source of our ideas, can we really be specific?

Lest all this begin to sound too apocalyptic, let me tell you about a lady who brushes her teeth with Gleem. She says her choice of Gleem has nothing whatever to do with television, because she pays no attention to commercials and is in no way influenced by them. When asked why she uses Gleem, then, she promptly answers that she has to use it because she can't brush after every meal.

I have been trying to suggest that the communication overload of our time, a product of the industrial revolution, has produced a fierce competition for attention and a tone contrasting sharply with that of two centuries ago. Television has become the epitome of the competitive tone. Even within the medium, competition between different genres, between different interests, has tended to make them similar. In all, a popular mythology provides the cohesive framework for information and ideas.

If one measures the success of a medium by the attention it commands, American television has been successful beyond belief. It was scarcely a half century ago that its first crude images flickered in the laboratory. Today advertisers are ready to spend more than $100,000 for 30 seconds of time during a Superbowl telecast. Considering the implications of such a pricetag and the willingness of sponsors to pay it, we can only describe the medium as one of the most amazing successes in history. Surely it is, up to the present moment, the high-water mark of the media revolution. But it is time to suggest that a price has been paid for this success. The bright tube, holding audiences spellbound, has helped to create unprecedented levels of consumption—a standard of living often called the highest in the world but that is now widely seen as involving dangerous liabilities.

To the extent that the assumptions and premises that underlie the success have seeped into our habits of thought they may have detracted from our ability to handle the problems now confronting us.

We face an energy crisis. Television the unparalleled merchandiser—of more powerful cars, of living better electrically, of the needless made necessary, of wasteful packaging, of planned obsolescence—television in its very successes would seem to be edging us further toward that crisis.

The world faces turmoil and violence. Our television has constantly promoted the mythology of a hero-villain world where problems have law-and-order solutions; it has successfully exported that mythology to a hundred other countries. How this may affect the behavior of people is not a matter that yields to precise research, for it would now be impossible to find a control group immune to television influences. But when a medium apparently affects, throughout much of the world, hair styles, clothing styles, vocabulary, the songs people sing and the drinks they drink, it is difficult to imagine why other kinds of behavior should be exempt. Again, the success may pose a problem.

We face an environmental crisis. The life-support system of our planet is threatened by pollution of the air, land, and water. At the same time, we use resources at a rate that spells possible disaster in the next century. Again television, as the apostle of the ever-greater growth rate, the gospel of plenty, may itself pose a problem.

Discussion of all these problems is assuming an increasing urgency. Such discussion cannot avoid questions about the future of media.

It so happens that at this juncture of history, laboratory developments point to new upheavals in communication—and to a possible new stage in the media revolution.

During recent years, cable television has spread rapidly, because it could bring into the home more channels than are possible in over-the-air television. In the not-too-distant future, this capability seems likely to experience a quantum jump, thanks to a thin glass fiber that looks like a violin string. A laser beam can travel through such fibers, carrying innumerable streams of communication simultaneously in both directions. Far more versatile than present coaxial cables, they seem likely to become the basis for wired cities and wired nations, linked worldwide via satellite. What does all this mean?

The scientist foresees wide change. He considers it likely that in a decade or two a citizen will be able, through pushbutton controls, to summon onto his home screen not only current events, drama, and sports such as are now available but also a wide range of other items. He might summon onto his screen a classic film, which a computerized switching system would at once call forth from a tape library. Or he might decide on a university course, likewise stored in an electronic repository. Each lesson, when needed, could be summoned by pushbutton. The optical fiber would also permit two-way communication. There could be meetings or seminars in which people in widely scattered locations would confer together, each seeing the others on a split television screen. The home screen might also have a printout adjunct so that supplementary documents, or newspapers, or graphic materials of various kinds could come spilling out. The citizen might also summon information from a computerized data bank.

Some of the services available to him might be sponsored, as in today's television, while others might involve a fee. In other words, some might be audience supported.

That such possibilities are within reach many experimenters and scholars seem to take for granted. They are far less in agreement on the social implications.

Let's look at a few predictions. Some sociologists feel it will be a democratizing development. They point out that heretofore an American family watching television has generally had a choice of three networks, all similarly financed and programmed. At times public television has been an important alternative, but its distribution has been spotty. An M.I.T. sociologist, Ithiel de Sola Pool, feels that the system has been a "powerful force toward conformity." Throughout the United States, he has written, "the same fads, the same styles, the same scandal of the week, the same ball scores, the same entertainments are on people's lips." He feels the future technology can help to "individualize people rather than homogenize them." He predicts: "Increasingly, communication devices will be adapted to individualized use by the consumer where and when he wants, on his own, without the cooperation of others; he will use machines as an extension of his own capabilities and personality, talking and listening worldwide, picking up whatever information he wants." Pool attaches special importance to the possibilities of interactive, two-way communication. An era in which the citizen "hears but is not heard" will be replaced, he feels, by an era of "citizen feedback." He apparently feels that the multiplicity of channels will reduce dependence on sponsors and end their dominant role.[7]

Against this optimism, there are opinions in an opposite direction. Decades ago, when Nazi Germany and Soviet Russia were reported to be developing wired-radio systems, these were at once assumed by Americans to be instruments for control—not liberation, not democratization. Why, when *we* develop a wired system, do we look on it as liberation? Obviously a wired system offers new control points and creates new gatekeepers. In addition, some people wonder whether a multiplicity of channels necessarily leads to diversity. Did a multiplicity of radio channels bring diversity, or an endless choice of stations playing the "top 40" hits? Some also foresee psychological problems in the wired city—an increasing isolation of the individual, a "lonely crowd" getting lonelier. And a Swedish psychologist, Marianne Franken-haeuser, suggests that a multiplicity of attractive choices can actually have a sort of paralyzing effect, impairing the ability to make decisions. As for the element of two-way communication, this seemed to the writer George Orwell the ultimate attack on privacy. With a two-way system, the viewer can become the viewed. This was part of the nightmare predicted in the novel *1984*.[8]

Nightmare or utopia, which will it be? Both would seem possible. And perhaps that is the reason for the rise of interest in problems of communication. It is only in this age of mass communication that communication has become a problem. Studies of influences, of control points, of gatekeepers, of unspoken premises, of subliminal seductions all acquire an urgency they never had. Our message therefore might be: users of Gleem, become aware.

That there will be continued upheavals in media—thanks to cables, optical fibers, cassettes, computers, satellites, laser beams—seems inevitable. The media revolution will go on. But that, as our symposium subtitle suggests, calls also for a continuing commitment. The revolution can have a democratic or a totalitarian direction. The result is not settled. It is not written in a sealed envelope, certified by Price Waterhouse, so that we need only say, "The envelope, please." No, the outcome is an unsettled matter, in which public knowledge and awareness can play a part.

Notes

[1] Frank Luther Mott, *American Journalism: A History of Newspapers in the United States Through 250 Years, 1690 to 1940* (New York: Macmillan, 1941) is the classic chronicle on the subject. For a vivid account of early advertising see Frank Spencer Presbrey, *The History and Development of Advertising* (New York: Doubleday, Doran, 1929).

[2] Alfred McClung Lee, *The Daily Newspaper in America; the Evolution of a Social Instrument* (New York: Macmillan, 1937).

[3] For reactions, pro and con, to the early motion picture craze, see Lewis Jacobs, *The Rise of the American Film; a Critical History* (New York: Harcourt, Brace, 1939). On the rise of radio broadcasting see Erik Barnouw, *A Tower in Babel* (New York: Oxford University Press, 1966).

[4] Wilbur Schramm, with Jack Lyle and Edwin Parker, *Television in the Lives of Our Children* (Stanford, Calif.: Stanford University Press, 1961). For a more recent work see Robert M.

Liebert, with John M. Neale and Emily S. Davidson, *The Early Window: Effects of Television on Children and Youth* (New York: Pergamon Press, 1973).

[5] On the "telefilm" as journalism see Erik Barnouw, *Tube of Plenty: the Evolution of American Television* (New York: Oxford University Press, 1975).

[6] The Shayon comments are in *Saturday Review*, November 19, 1966. For government as show business see Newton N. Minow, with John Bartlow Martin and Lee M. Mitchell, *Presidential Television* (New York: Basic Books, 1973). For a seminal discussion of the subject see Daniel J. Boorstin, *The Image: A Guide to Pseudo-Events in America* (New York: Atheneum, 1971).

[7] Ithiel de Sola Pool, comp., *Talking Back: Feedback and Cable Technology* (Cambridge, Mass.: MIT Press, 1974). For an early optimistic forecast see Harold J. Barnett and Edward Greenberg, *A Proposal for Wired City Television* (Santa Monica Calif.: Rand Corporation, 1967).

[8] Marianne Frankenhaeuser, *Man in Technological Society; Stress, Adaptation, and Tolerance Limits* (Stockholm: University of Stockholm, 1974). George Orwell, *Nineteen Eighty-Four: A Novel* (New York: Harcourt, Brace, 1949).

W. McNeil Lowry received a bachelor's degree in English from the University of Illinois in 1934. He stayed at Illinois for graduate work and in 1942 was awarded the Ph.D. in English. He was a faculty member there in the English Department from 1936 to 1942, when he left Urbana to go into the United States Navy. After the war, he was chief for the Washington Bureau of the James M. Cox newspapers. He left Washington to become associate director of the International Press Institute in Zurich before joining the staff of the Ford Foundation in 1953. Dr. Lowry served in many capacities at the Ford Foundation. First, he was director of the foundation's education program, then director of its program in the humanities and the arts, and then he was vice-president in charge of the foundation's Office of Policy and Planning. In his last several years at the foundation, he was vice-president with special responsibility for the Division of the Humanities and the Arts.

The Arts in America

Evolution and Tradition

W. McNEIL LOWRY

UNTIL ROUGHLY THE MIDPOINT of the 19th century, the arts in the United States continued to be largely derivative of Western Europe, with literature—more than the musical or visual arts—the key medium of transmission or, here and there, of transmutation. The other strong cultural influence—the speech and the song of Africans—had been felt in a large area of the country for more than a hundred years, but the white majority were as yet unconscious of its real impact. The first American artists of international standard were writers and New Englanders.

But even before the end of the 18th century, political and social forces had begun to exert their influence and to prepare the way for an ultimately indigenous culture. At the risk of drastic oversimplification, the most important of these factors were the doctrine of toleration (and therefore of dissent) and the movement of culture on the ever-westward frontier. North America had been colonized through a complex of economic and social motivations. One segment was composed of landlords expanding their holdings, another was of either indentured or penniless persons selling their own labor. Still another was of particular religious-cum-social sects looking for toleration but on the new continent often restricting toleration of others. At the bottom were the slaves, who constituted only property or wealth for their owners. The movement toward dissent and the frontiersman's quest for his own stake in the society in their different ways came to symbolize movements against the Establishment, whether political or religious. Of more significance to the cultural history of the United States was a concomitant evolution in the language of the people that ultimately prepared the way for naturalism and realism. Shakespeare, the translators of the King James Bible, and John Bunyan were only a part of the cultural influences on a Thomas Jefferson. To a lesser extent this was also true of the New Englanders and the Virginians who, with the Anglican church as an instrument, planted educational institutions west of the Alleghenies. To the pioneer himself, they were the sum of cultural heritage. There grew up a particular blend of declamatory rhetoric, metaphor, and concrete imagery which ultimately would divide and distinguish the American from his British antecedents, particularly when there was added to it the rhythmic intervals of the black who now had forgotten any language but his own dialect of English. Biblical rhetoric, the metaphor of Bunyan, and concrete imagery were equally visible in Melville, but the symbols were deeply psychological. In almost the same era those of Mark Twain were rooted in everyday life. A great divide had begun to open up between the cultural idiom of the indigenous American and that of his English forebears.

By the same midpoint of the century there was a cultural schism in the United States itself. Musical and dramatic groups from Europe pushed beyond the Hudson and helped much later to stimulate the establishment of operatic or symphonic organizations in the centers of river traffic, particularly those settled by Germans. Like the cultural organizations of New York and Boston, these were often considered by most either as symbols of a largely Eastern establishment or alien and formal temples in which it was hard to be oneself. Though there was a thin line of American drama and American opera beginning even in the 18th century, the repertoire of touring companies was thoroughly European.

But in the meantime, again through the medium of literature, an indigenous American naturalism or realism was unfolding, and contrary to popular impression it was not confined to the West. In the East it was visible even as early as Cooper and Irving, was graphically exhibited by Howells, and by the turn of the century was to turn the principal works of Wharton and James to complex analyses of cultural conflict between upper-class Americans and their English or continental counterparts. What was significant about realism in the American West was that the language forged by the writer of fiction—rhetorical, even bombastic, rhythmic, humorous, self-deprecating, down to earth—was suited as an instrument of popular culture and an increasingly populist society. Unconsciously Samuel Clemens, Bret Harte, Willa Cather, and others prepared the way for the political novel of Frank Norris in which the Establishment, social or corporate, was the villain. The same political climate was shortly to produce the individual income tax of 1913 and the inheritance tax of 1916, which, if they increased the importance of private patrons in the development of the arts in the United States, did so by spreading the patron's role far beyond a few proud possessors and ultimately fashioned vehicles which opened artistic control to the artists themselves.

For many American artists the 20th century began in 1913, not primarily because of the Armory Show and its impact upon painting and sculpture but because it was the last year before a World War blew away 19th-century Europe. Whether in Chicago or in New York or expatriate in Paris, the American artist felt a present and a future and did not feel bereft of a past. If the American artist felt misprized by his society, so did his British counterpart. Dreiser, the Muckrakers, and Mencken in their different ways not only swung at the Establishment but took art out of the drawing room. First painting and then the drama moved into the streets and looked into the ashcans. Though social democracy advanced slowly and was as often set back, the middle class and not merely the rich were challenged to reexamine their values and mores, and the common man became the subject not only of pathos but of tragedy. By the midpoint of the century the avant garde would convert him into the antihero.

The American artist, in sum, felt a social role, if only that of a critic or rebel. In the same period he began to feel something equally important to the cultural development of the United States. This was the opportunity, however difficult to seize, to organize an artistic group for his own and other artists' careers. In the history of civilization, such an opportunity has rarely existed, even for great artists with princely patrons. To set the goals of an artistic enterprise, the artist normally had to get to the top of an institution belonging to the state. In the United States, a young country slow to develop government patronage of the arts, social and political mechanisms afforded the possibility of control by one or more artists or voluntary associations of artists and their friends. The artist himself did not have the money by which to utilize these mechanisms, but he no longer had to be dependent upon the whims of a single wealthy patron. If the artist were both talented and aggressive he could often exert control. Sometimes a producer or manager who shared his artistic goals used his own money and that of his more cultivated friends.

Many other unrelated factors in the 20th century stimulated the development of new groups and institutions in the arts and concentrated the creative energies for which they were the outlets. The closing of the last frontiers on the American continent caused subsequent generations to direct their energies elsewhere. Families only a generation or so from the pioneers sought to memorialize both their own names and the communities founded by their fathers; education, health, and culture all benefited. Those new patrons who cared little about aesthetic experiences for themselves often felt they were somehow important to the education of their children. Many state legislatures took the same tentative view. It is noteworthy that the state universities, originally dedicated to agricultural and mechanical laborers, became the first to teach the practice—in addition to the theory and history— of the arts.

By the thirties another influence had been felt. In earlier centuries, hardly any of the political refugees leaving Europe for America had been noted artists. Now these came in large numbers. By 1940 New York had become the international capital for painting, sculpture, music, and dance. But perhaps more lasting in influence was the fertilization of conservatories, schools of art, orchestras, and universities across the country.

Yet with all these manifestations the arts in the United States were in many ways underdeveloped. Both the creative and the performing artist lacked sufficient established outlets. Many performers, dependent only on commercial managers or producers, could not really train themselves in the basic reper- toire. The Second World War ended with little change in the national pattern, but it was a pattern that within another decade was to break up.

Before looking at the period of most rapid evolution in an American tra- dition, we need to characterize the tradition itself, if indeed any charac- terization is possible. What, after all, is generically American beyond its simple comparison or contrast with the European? Equally simple, though real enough, is the concept of a cultural melting pot. As a society, the United States even by now has seen not only the fusion of national or ethnic influences into a single American idiom but the survival of specific ethnic or national cultures alongside the common matrix, so that many Americans express at one and the same time two cultures.

Is there, however, anything uniquely American, and if there is, has it the force of a tradition? It has frequently been said that the uniqueness of Ameri- can life is the American's consciousness of the very concept of uniqueness. This may appear to be like winning an argument without having it, but it nevertheless fairly characterizes the American's view of himself and of the world. It comprehends almost all the things that, for better or worse, are taken by both Americans and foreigners to be typically American—our sense of mission, our view of history as progressive rather than retrospective and our own society as the laboratory, our fantasy that the eyes of the world are constantly upon us.

In his first inaugural address, James Monroe proclaimed:

Never did a Government commence under auspices so favorable, nor ever was success so complete. If we look to the history of other Nations, ancient or modern, we find no example of a growth so rapid–so gigantic; of a people so prosperous, and happy . . . . the heart of every citizen must expand with joy, when he reflects how near our Government has approached to perfection; that, in respect to it, we have no essential improvement to make . . . .

If the immigrants who came in successive waves in the 19th century were somewhat less complacent than Monroe about their situation in the New World, they nevertheless shared the belief that they were uniquely favored. Despite the obvious stratification into economic and social classes forced upon most of them in an industrializing America, they persisted in adopting the American faith in social mobility, if not for themselves then for their children.

From pre-Revolutionary times onward, expressions of the distinctive American sense of destiny, of mission, of uniqueness comprehended both the philosophical and the materialistic, the sacred and the mundane. And it is exactly in this compound that one must locate the fixed dilemma in America's commitment to the arts. On the one hand, both art and the artist are made to appear as secondary to another goal—education, social uplift, urban renewal, business itself. On the other, the artist himself is often led to feel an alien in a materialistic society, though he may be entranced by its profusion. "Puritanism and Big Business" an astute foreign observer once entitled his analysis of the American culture. In a young country with a manifest destiny blessed by Providence, the theme of alienation emerged surprisingly early.

Voluntary societies, the importance of which to the American Republic has so long been recognized, made the first organized commitments to the arts. In 1804 a group of artists and their friends in Philadelphia collected works of art to aid in the training of painters and sculptors. Retrospectively the Pennsylvania Academy of Fine Arts, though established more than a century before income and inheritance taxes, has become a symbol of the device by which private patrons helped to develop artistic groups and institutions. Before the First World War, however, private patronage was restricted to those wealthy enough to contribute directly from their incomes. Art museums, symphony orchestras, and opera companies benefited largely, singers and instrumentalists indirectly, creative artists very little. Theater and the concert stage were under the control of commercial managers. Dance was barely beginning to stir.

As previously noted, a reform in tax legislation in 1913 and 1916 became the means of widening the number of artistic patrons beyond the very rich. Neither President Wilson nor the Congress saw the legislation as a historic commitment to the arts, however. It is characteristic of our entire history that its language referred to educational, scientific, and charitable—but not artistic or cultural—institutions. So far as the tax collectors were concerned, the arts were still secondary rather than primary ends. Fortunately, the revenue agents did not try to define which artistic creation was educational and which was not, though a later amendment provided higher tax deductions for gifts to institutions or enterprises that were totally educational.

Following the inheritance tax, more great personal fortunes became the endowments of national philanthropic foundations. In the main these again looked at the arts as a means to education or even as frivolous and unworthy objects of the philanthropic dollar. Only after the midcentury did this begin to change, conspicuously in the multimillion-dollar program of artistic patronage from the Ford Foundation. A change in the taxes on excess profits of corporations produced the same result. Corporations took advantage of the new provisions only very slowly, and education and health were the beneficiaries. Only in this decade have corporations begun to pay a little more attention to the arts, partly through corporate gifts and partly through institutional advertising.

In the introductory section of this paper I noted a few of the factors which stimulated a change in national patterns affecting the arts after World War II. The arts as an ethic or aesthetic took on a new doctrinal urgency in many diverse segments of the society. Among many other claims, the arts were said to be:

- important to the image of the American society abroad
- a means of communication and consequently of understanding between this country and others
- an expression of national purpose
- an important influence in the liberal education of the individual
- an important key to an American's understanding of himself, his times, and his destiny
- a purposeful occupation for youth
- in their institutional form, vital to the social, moral, and educational resources of an American community
- therefore good for business, especially in new centers of population
- components for strengthening moral and spiritual bastions in a people whose national security might be threatened
- an offset to the materialism of a generally affluent society.

Note that the arguments advanced for the arts in the fifties almost totally accepted their role as a means to some other end. It is equally noteworthy that many of the proponents of these claims were busy translating their interest in the arts into buildings—a rash of cultural centers across the country. The so-called "cultural explosion" of the fifties and sixties was in great part promotional. Though on an absolute scale there was more financial support being made available for the arts, it was not always channeled into artistic enterprises meeting the criteria of quality. Artists resigned themselves to the probability that new money in the arts might first reflect itself in bigger college programs, new activities for schoolchildren, and new halls for performances. Some were bitter that the outlets for professional careers in many fields remained woefully inadequate. There were conflicting judgments among artists concerning the satisfaction to be derived from teaching, but there was universal discouragement over the fact that teaching remained the principal economic base for professionals in some of the important fields.

Despite these mixed prospects, the fifties and early sixties witnessed more sweeping changes in the institutional base of the arts than any other period in our history. And artistic directors and producers, using the instrument of the tax-exempt corporation, were enabled to maintain a significant degree of control. This was particularly true of those who had taken independent initiative in the establishment of individual companies. It was less true of those who depended from the start on initiative from laymen banding together to support a new artistic enterprise in their own communities.

In a development without historical precedent, the strategy was adopted of using particular models to inform the creation of additional artistic institutions. In the process, and indeed as a necessary precondition, artistic directors were brought out of their isolation to share experiences and ways of doing things. Private philanthropy permitted many of them also to experiment with new ways, to open new avenues of significance to an entire field. When these appeared especially promising, technical assistance was added for a concentrated effort, as in methods by which to build larger and more permanent audiences for performing arts groups.

The changes went so far that the institutional base and even the economics of particular art fields were permanently altered. At the beginning of the period the commercial theater in New York dominated the whole field, save for about a dozen winter stock companies around the country. By the mid-sixties resident professional companies outside New York employed more Equity actors over significant segments of a season than did the entire commercial theater in New York and on the road. In the same period more new jobs for professional dancers were created in existing and newly formed ballet companies than had been available in the whole field in 1950. The outlets for young opera singers expanded in the same proportion. And in all three fields, plus that of symphonic music, the seasons for which performers were contracted steadily lengthened. In the concert field the university and college system greatly expanded audiences for the performer.

The currents which ran in this period were felt nationally—but often only in retrospect. Curiously enough, some of the artistic producers most caught up in them did not foresee the results, though this may not be totally surprising given the fact that everything happened within little more than a decade. There was little feeling of nationalism involved, and by no means so much regionalism as the daily press came to allege. One measure is to be found in the repertoire. American painting was the one conspicuous exception, as it came to dominate the international style. Repertoire in the performing arts was a blend of the classical and of 20th-century European and American, save of course for modern dance, on which any European influence had always been negligible.

Strengthening existing institutions and forming new ones did, however, give increased importance to the new work beyond the commercial impulse of the Broadway hit and even in defiance of the assumed prejudices of the buyers at the box office. Some artistic producers were as interested in new works by Europeans as in those by Americans. But by the early sixties almost all were at least on the defensive about the production of new works by Americans. Organized private philanthropy played a new and significant role through efforts to give visibility to the careers of creative artists. And some of the small experimental groups which sprang up in this period were totally devoted to new works by Americans.

Enlarging the institutional base has had an effect on style and repertoire that has been little noted, perhaps because the chief media for criticism are still largely centered in New York. The principal effect has been on the speed with which the avant garde or the experimental is transformed into standard repertoire. The theater may be taken as an example. The movement from Pirandello through Ionesco, Beckett, Pinter, and Albee to the new British and American playwrights would have been far different if it had depended upon the original New York productions. Their works went immediately into the professional resident companies around the country, not for one production but as a permanent part of the repertoire. Another strong influence on the American drama, the works of Brecht, depended solely upon the non-profit companies. The few New York productions of Brecht have almost without exception been disasters.

In the cultural history of any country or any age, it is normally true that personal influences are attributed to creative artists and a few glamorous or charismatic performers rather than to artistic producers or entrepreneurs. In 20th-century Europe Diaghilev, Stanislavski, and Beecham were some of the few exceptions to this rule. In America personal influences were normally attached to writers, painters, composers, and a few actors and singers. In the fifties and sixties, when the whole institutional structure was expanding, the artistic director attained a degree of influence—though not of fame—rivaling or surpassing that of the creative artist. This was not a conscious or concerted movement, however, and it was not generally understood even by those who participated in it. The artistic director or producer felt thoroughly engaged, or even overburdened, in the effort to build a nonprofit professional institution and to preserve it to an uncertain future. In the process he or she inevitably discovered peers who were similarly engaged. It was only with a measure of distrust and disbelief that they ever joined one another in a common effort to relate social and economic forces to their own goals. They could not really believe in their own influence. Outside their own institution they generally left initiative to motivated laymen, though recognizing that the motives of these varied in their impact on professional and artistic goals. But however wary they were of joint action or the ambitions of their peers, they now recognized an inevitable kind of fraternity on a national basis, albeit loose and scattered. This was a new feeling for artistic directors and producers in America; artistic fraternities hitherto had involved artists in a particular discipline or within particular salons and academies.

The increasing demarcation between the nonprofit and commercial corporation tightened the common bond. The new ranks in the theater, for example, at first felt patronized by commercial producers, agents, artists' managements, and the artist unions, but in the sixties the tables began to turn. When in the early seventies there was a temporary slump on Broadway, commercial producers staged a largely unsuccessful raid on public and private patronage. They proclaimed a "First American Congress in the Theatre," at which the podium was usurped by their most intemperate critics.

We require a longer historical perspective even to speculate on what might have happened had the artists themselves, led by the directors of companies and institutions, staked out the terms of a national policy and drawn a clear line between ends and means. It is of course taking advantage of hindsight to say that the decade before President Johnson signed the National Foundation bill was a peculiarly opportune time for such an effort. And there were many voices raised. As I have noted, however, many of these subordinated the artist and the arts while appearing to promote them.

The advent of federal support in 1965, a historic step in America's potential commitment to the arts, might have been expected to raise the whole question to the level of public policy. But that has not happened, at least to this date. Indeed the federal program in the arts expresses the permanent dilemma in the American commitment. With one hand the National Endowment for the Arts attempts to help in the annual maintenance of professional groups or institutions. With the other it subordinates the professional to educational or community goals. Thus it has, broadly, two constituencies, though each contains variations within it. One is made up of artistic directors and managers, the other largely comprises educators and laymen. Inevitably a contest has arisen not only over the proportion of funds to each but over the policies implicit in such a division. Should federal patronage be designed to preserve professional activities of proved or potential artistic quality? Should it be devoted to community projects and extracurricular programs for school-children? In either case, what is the influence on private patronage, upon which professional groups and institutions must continue to depend?

The decade in which federal patronage finally began also saw the rise of the counterculture, which had its own influences on the quality of the American commitment to the arts. It was not one influence. Some young creative or performing artists wanted not only to perfect their craft and technique but to communicate more directly to their audience. They wanted to feel something coming back to them from other human beings in the process. They wanted to be not virtuosi but educators or communicants. They attacked elitism and they attacked the cultural establishment, but they wanted at the same time to be artists.

Others—and they were the majority—attacked elitism and the Establishment under the banner of "participation." But to them anything that even existed, however struggling, was the Establishment. Performers and audience were participants in a communion, and the only thing that mattered was the event. One style or one technique was as good as another. The fields most affected were popular music, modern dance, theatre, and the multimedia. In its own way the counterculture contributed to amateurism and the blurring of artistic standards as directly as did the proponents of the arts as a means to purely social and educational ends. Many Americans began to think that the arts were somehow a panacea for youth and that creativity was to be found only among those who had not reached the age of 30. And their activities cost much less than was required by professional ensembles. A major share of the funds from state arts councils appears to be based on this principle.

The danger of elitism is really less than that of amateurism at this stage in the development of the arts in America. Professional outlets for artists and their creations were never more numerous nor their audiences more unlimited. Until quite recently no one—historian, philosopher, the artist himself—would have foreseen a time when the arts would occupy a central position in reflecting or expressing American life and American social values. But no sooner is this cultural phenomenon revealed than it is immediately generalized to embrace all activities in the name of art. A contest over patronage leading to the scatteration of funds could mean a qualitative reduction in artistic institutions, just as the leveling of public funds to include community colleges has already impaired higher education.

The potential effect could be quite serious for other reasons also. The professional institutions and companies that have consolidated their position since the fifties are the source of training and experience for developing talents. The whole question of professional and craft training is being taken more seriously than at any other time in our cultural history. And there have been real achievements in extending career opportunities for performers, conspicuously in opera, theater, and dance. With the organized assistance of private philanthropy, opera companies around the country have finally made it possible for the most talented young singers to choose equally between the United States and Europe.

Not unrelated to the increased emphasis upon professional training resources is a growing consciousness of aesthetic form and discipline on the part of the audience, particularly the best educated. In effect, it represents both a reaction against the counterculture and a sympathetic impulse toward something controlled and disciplined in a solipsistic and threatened age. It accounts for another quantum jump in the American audience for ballet and relates indirectly to a greater depth of content and design in contemporary painting and music. But the creative manifestations which induce it are dependent upon those professional companies and groups contesting for patronage with the amateur and his official or officious spokesmen.

I noted in my introduction to this paper that some American artists came to feel themselves in a social role, even if only as critic or rebel. This feeling, of course, is characteristic of artists as a species and not merely of those in a particular national tradition. But the American artist over the last generation has added another dimension.

To a degree unique in advanced societies, American artists and artistic directors influence the creation and preservation of companies and institutions as much as, or even more than, do their financial patrons. This is just another example of the sense of purpose open to the American. But the result is that the artist often feels not only that his personal goals are in conflict with the utilitarian or materialistic spirit in U.S. society but that the artistic groups and institutions he wants to build are threatened by that spirit.

That is why a contest over a national policy about the arts is even more acute in the United States than in other countries with a long tradition of public patronage. This is also why, in the long run, sweeping compromises over the subordination of the arts to social or educational ends could be fateful. We cannot completely rule out the future prospect that the artist may have to reject even those who appear in the role of his advocates. America's commitment to the arts will finally be judged by our ability to discriminate. It is easier to popularize the arts than to repress them, and the one fate may therefore be more crucial than the other.

After I had agreed to perform this function of introducing the speakers, a trouble-some problem crossed my mind. I said to my wife, "How in the world does one introduce Margaret Mead?" I first heard of Margaret Mead about 1938, when I read Coming of Age in Samoa *as an undergraduate assignment. Since then with increasing frequency, particularly in the last 20 years or so, one comes across her almost every month. We read her articles, both learned and popular, or read a review of one of her books and sometimes the book itself, or we see an interview with her or a quotation from her in a magazine or newspaper, or we see her on Professor Barnouw's tube. Her name has become a household word. She truly is a person who does not need an introduction. This one will be brief.*

Dr. Mead graduated from Barnard in 1923 and received an M.A. the following year from Columbia. She took the Ph.D. at Columbia in 1929, where she did her graduate work with Franz Boas and Ruth Benedict. She began her career with the American Museum of Natural History in 1926 as assistant curator of ethnology in the Museum's Department of Anthropology. She stayed with the museum until she retired—that is, retired from the museum—for in no sense is she really retired. She has written 24 books. Coming of Age in Samoa *was the first in 1928. Two of her recent ones have received special attention: her biography of Ruth Benedict, which appeared two years ago, and her autobiographical* Blackberry Winter: My Earlier Years, *published in 1972. She also has been coauthor or coeditor of 18 other books, and perhaps not even she knows how many monographs and articles she has written.*

Awards and honorary degrees abound. She has received 20 honorary degrees and such awards as the Ceres Medal of the United Nations Food and Agricultural Organization and the Woman of Conscience Award from the National Council of Women. Time *magazine in 1969 even named her "Mother of the World."*

Styles of American Womanhood Through 200 Years of History*

MARGARET MEAD

Mr. Chairperson, ladies and gentlemen and scholars. In talking about a historical theme I think that I have to explain that I am not a historian. I don't expect to be excoriated on any solid historical grounds because I am approaching my theme from a very different stance, from having spent a good portion of my life among primitive people watching the relationships between men and women and children in societies where people live the way our ancestors lived ten or twenty thousand years ago—depending upon who we are. Those of us who have a pure Anglo-Saxton ancestry, as they sometimes call it in Virginia, may of course be historically closer to some of these primitive peoples than some other people here. But nevertheless it makes a considerable difference whether one is working with a stance that looks at our history as the most important thing that ever happened or sees the 200 years of our history against a background that began in Greece and ended with us, whether one looks at the whole history of civilization and sees the American experience as part of the history of civilization, or whether one places it against several thousand years of human history. This means that one looks at people very differently.

And I'm going to be looking at some themes in the lives of American women from the faraway position of primitive women, on the one hand, and also in relation to the world that we are moving into and how the kind of people we are now fits us to be the kind of people that we are going to have to

* Edited transcript of an address delivered without notes

become if we are to fit into that later world. Now the statements that I'm going to make are the kind that anthropologists make. For instance, when we say the necktie is a feature of American male dress, somebody comes along and says "But lots of American men don't wear neckties." The answer is: "That's just what I mean." Not wearing a necktie in the United States is very different from not wearing a necktie in New Guinea. Every single male in this country is either wearing a necktie or not wearing a necktie, and they're all related to neckties. It's that sort of statement that I'm going to make. The next statement, you know—how many people wear neckties, members of which classes wear neckties, whether or not you can get into a Hilton hotel dining room without a necktie—all these are minor details that have to be worked out by a very different method, but I'll be discussing things in this rather broad fashion, that is, in the same way that we catagorize the grammar of a language, for instance. People speak a language very differently, but it is not very difficult to discover whether people are speaking French or English, even if they are drunk or senile or making love or talking to the baby. You can still tell whether its French or English. And it is in those general terms that I'll be talking.

Also I have to say that I have not studied Americans, either past or present, in the same way that I've studied the people that I looked at very closely in New Guinea or in Bali or in Samoa, where for a period of months or years one lives in a village as intensively as the people who live in that village all their lives. There have been some peculiar instances when people have asked me when I went back to a New Guinea village after 25 years, "Did anyone remember you?" And the other part of the question is, "Did you remember anybody?" Now, of course, they remembered what I ate for breakfast every single day the whole time I was there, whether I stepped on one bank of the river or the other, and who was in the second canoe behind us at a wedding in another village. I was such an unusual event in their village life that they absorbed me as they absorbed the memory of everything that happened to them. And I remember them equally well because I was there to study them.

As far as America is concerned, I've not worked in the same way, though I've spent a certain amount of time on other studies that are being done in this country, but my major material on America is that I am an American. I'm a 10th-generation American and I was very close to my grandmother, which put me a hundred years back in a small town in Ohio and I still keep up with about 50 assorted relatives, so that I keep a running relationship to America, but in terms of the understandings that I learned in New Guinea. So I'll ask you to remember that I am always talking, in a sense, from a distance and that I'm always conscious of that distance. I'm very conscious, for instance, in looking at an audience like this, that there are no children. Now this isn't as odd as it would be at a women's club; a women's club with no children is transcendently odd. Once you put some men in the audience it doesn't look so strange not to have some children. But nevertheless, to be addressing a group of adults only is something that I always feel strangely conscious of, that we segregate people out for certain kinds of occasions and put in or cut out so many other people who would be there under other circumstances.

What I want to think primarily about today is what the division of labor in this country has been, because when we look at all the earlier societies we find that the primary division of labor has been between men and women, right through human history. There are great variations as a society becomes more complex, but nevertheless the division of labor between men and women —what were men's tasks and what were women's tasks, no matter how much a man could, in an emergency, take on a woman's task or a woman a man's— has been the basis of the way we've handled the organization of our lives for a very, very long time. At present we are proposing, as a society—and that's not only in the United States, of course, but in Western Europe and many other parts of the world—we're proposing for the first time in human history to obliterate that division of labor. That proposal is an exceedingly important one. We weren't able to make such a proposal on any very large scale until the population explosion, which meant that it was no longer necessary for women to devote their entire lives to bearing and rearing children who would probably die in very large numbers. So the modern medical revolution and the population explosion have made it possible to create a new kind of world in which we are seriously proposing that one's sex should not determine one's occupation or one's role in society. Within that proposed change we have to think very hard about some of the things that have happened and are going to happen.

But I want to go back to the kind of division of labor we had in the original 13 colonies and in the early United States—back to the selection of the women who came to this country. I'll deal first with Europe, where at least people nominally made decisions of their own, even though they were driven out in political or religious persecutions. It has been demonstrated, when we've looked at the selection of immigrants from England, that in every group of people who decided to leave their home country and come to this country there were selections based on personality. A certain kind of girl was willing to come to America, another kind wanted to stay home with mother. The men, of course, were also selected as special kinds of people who were willing to make the trip across the Atlantic and try their fate in a new country; the ones who didn't feel very strongly about it stayed home with the girls who wanted to stay near their mothers. We had a very high selection for women who had some pretty definite characteristics. Again, remember that this statement is like my statement about neckties. There were, of course, all sorts of women who ended up here, but the common characteristic of all those women was bravery—and this continues to be true of the women or families who have fled from political persecution more recently. These women weren't frightened; they weren't afraid of facing new conditions; they weren't afraid of hardship; they weren't afraid that they might be left alone in some strange new place.

This last point is, I think, one of the very important things about American women. In all the early days of colonization, they knew that at any moment they might be left alone. They might be left alone because their husbands would die, and they'd be alone in a strange country. When their husbands went away, they might be left alone to fight the Indians. Of course, there weren't nearly enough Indians to go around to cover all the situations in which people thought they might be left alone to fight. But nevertheless, the idea that a woman might be left alone with her children to fight the Indians was very important. In fact, a few years ago I was getting a group of Kansans to discuss what made a house a real house as compared with a shanty or shack. They decided it was two doors, a front door and a back door. When you had two doors you had a house. And I asked what are the two doors for. They gave a completely American answer. They said you could go out the back door when the Indians came in the front.

We may look at what happened to the roles of women on farms in this country as compared with their roles in Europe. In Europe it was the women who milked the cows but in this country the barn was too far from the house and the Indians might be there. Men took over milking and milking became a male occupation. Anything becomes a prestigious occupation when men take it over. This is one of the generalities that one can make in every culture in the world: that whatever men do is achievement and whatever women do isn't very important because they, after all, have all those babies which are important and that ought to be enough for them. They shouldn't be claiming other kinds of achievement. In many parts of this country the farm garden was split in half: there was a little garden near the house which was close enough so the Indians wouldn't get there, where women could go out and pick a few things for dinner. But the truck patch was a long way off and belonged to the men. They plowed it and they looked after it. These are, of course, only examples of the sorts of changes that occurred in America.

One of the things that we notice in this country as compared with Britain—and this lasted into my childhood—is the style of the woman who didn't marry compared with that of the woman who did marry. In Britain a woman who didn't marry was stereotyped as masculine. She was a "father's sister." She preferred nephews and she kept tomcats. In this country, the woman who didn't marry was stereotyped as "mother's sister;" she liked nieces, she kept tabby cats, and lived with her sister, who was a good strong-minded person, the kind a man wanted to marry. This definition of the marriageable woman as a woman who could stand on her own feet, manage by herself, drive the horses if her husband had an accident as they were crossing the country in a covered wagon, able to take charge whenever it was necessary, has been a very strong element, I think, in the building of American female character.

The division of labor that had existed in Europe survived in these different forms as the woman had the domain in the house and the man had the domain outside the house. And this is, of course, universal. Everywhere in the world the inside of the house tends to belong to women more than to men, but in many parts of the world women don't make men as miserable as they succeed in making them in this country whenever men attempt to invade their domain. The general picture of the man who had to wipe his feet when he came into the house and the extent to which women ruled the domestic domain extended into the 1930's and 1940's in a very odd way. When women started to make money, to work outside the home, one of the things they talked about was *their* money. Now no man has ever been known to have any money of his own in this country if he was married. His money was assigned to the house and bringing up the children. But we had quite a period when women had their own money. It started with the chicken-and-egg money on the farm and moved up very often, when they had quite a responsible job of their own—when they worked outside their own domain. They were still independent, separate people, doing what they could do themselves and disposing of the money they made as they saw fit.

In many parts of the world the relationships between men and women are very highly complementary in the expectation of character, and women may be expected to be extremely different from men in many ways. In many societies, of course, women are supposed to exist primarily to relate to their husbands, to look after their husbands, feed their husbands, and bring up the children, and are supposed to have no life of their own that is not related very closely to the lives of husbands and fathers, who themselves are supposed to spend their entire lives supporting their households.

This has virtually never existed in this country. American women are not good wives, if you define a good wife as someone who alertly waits for a husband's step on the stairs and rushes for his slippers. We've had a minimum of rushing for slippers right straight through our history. The definition of the wife and mother that developed in the pioneering days and continues to develop whenever you have a group immigrating into this country is someone who has her own job to do inside the house and does it. It's a picture of a reasonable partnership with men (American women are, on the whole, quite good sports), but it has virtually no complementarity in it at all. She had her domain, he had his. He went out, she stayed in. She told him what he could do in the house, and he told her what she couldn't do outside the house. We have an amusing dramatization today of this division between the outdoors and the indoors which was so strong between men and women in this country— the outdoors including the barn and the truck patch. This is the argument over the garbage, which is a major point of friction in modern marriages. Garbage is ambiguous. Garbage originates indoors and goes outdoors. Who does it belong to?

So in the United States there has been a pretty high mutuality of roles in which persons were thought of as relatively complete human beings in themselves. And I think this is very important, because it has had many repercussions. We have almost no tolerance in this country for any person or group of people who are not autonomous, who aren't capable of being independent and able to look after themselves.

This has been rather hard on small children, because infants are not autonomous at birth, although American mothers treat children as if they were. They put them to sleep in a room with no light, close the door and say, "Now go to sleep," the equivalent of saying, "Now be independent." And they address them, almost from birth, in language appropriate, possibly, for a four-year-old: "Don't hit mother with that spoon. Don't you realize that if you hit mother with that spoon it will break mother's glasses?" And this apostrophizing starts very early. Children are pushed into being autonomous, independent little creatures. Of course, they're not very autonomous and they're not very good at it. But we're extremely impatient with children who are clinging and dependent and we've carried this to the state today where we are very impatient with any children that need any help from anybody. We are conspicuously unwilling to care for all our helpless and lost and handicapped and miserable children. And we've carried it over in the opposite direction toward old people. In societies where you have a complementary relationship between the sexes and a complementary relationship between parents and children, you also have a complementary relationship between old and young. First the old care for the young, and then the young care for the old.

But that's not the American style. The American style of relationships between generations is illustrated in a story my father used to tell me about an old bird that had a little bird in its beak and was carrying it across a river. And the old bird holding the little bird in his beak said, "My son, when I am old will you care for me?" And the little bird said, "No, father, but I'll care for my children as you've cared for me." So we want a minimum of complementarity or reciprocity between the generations. And so we find today millions of older people whose one aim in life is to preserve their independence, to not be dependent on anyone else. Of course, this gets translated into not doing anything for anyone else either. Not being dependent on someone else can be called "not spoiling my daughter's life." This is extended to a refusal to become part of any kind of interdependent relationship.

One of the first things that I think it is important to realize about American women is this independence, this sense of their capacity to manage things themselves, their ability to substitute for their husbands if their husbands are away. This is carried over into our willingness to elect widows to political office. We don't like "the President's wife" doing things. And one of the major problems of having a woman President in this country is what would we do with her husband. But we're willing for the widow of a governor or the widow of a senator or the widow of or wife of a governor who can't serve a second term to run instead. That is, women are allowed to substitute for men. And that means, of course, they're supposed to have the same kind of courage and endurance and toughness that men have. But they're not supposed to substitute for men unless it's necessary. And this was the general style with which we built home life in this country: that a woman should be able to work, able to look after the children, able to run the farm all by herself, able to look after a plantation in the South, sometimes an enormous plantation with a large number of slaves. She might be left there all alone to manage the whole plantation. I think it's necessary also to consider whether the statement that I'm making about strong women was true of people who came here against their will. But as far as we can tell the slave ships, where only the very strong survived the passage, as well as conditions in the early days of slavery in this country, also promoted the survival of strong women who were able to manage on their own.

When women emerged from the home in this country, there again were stylized ways in which they were allowed to do this. On the frontier, we had two kinds of women. One of the peculiar things in this country, of course, is the way the good people and the bad people kept getting mixed up. I once heard Daniel Boorstin give a very interesting lecture on the way in which the bad man becomes the sheriff at the drop of a hat in this country. In the 1940's we had a type of film heroine who was called "the good bad girl" because she looked as if she were bad but turned out to be good. She had to do quite a few things to look bad. And the picture in the frontier town was, on one hand, of the strong, generous, bad woman who wasn't very bad. She was loose, but nevertheless she was generous. She kept people in order, she looked after them, she fed them, she put them to bed when they were drunk—and she could always reform and become a good woman. All she had to do was be made an honest woman of. And she could change almost overnight. And then on the other hand there was the good woman who arrived on the frontier and cleaned up the town (of whom, of course, Carry Nation is a very good instance). These women left the home for the outside world, taking the virtues of the home with them, and went out to battle for prohibition, to battle against slavery, to battle for women's rights, and so forth. The home was the launching platform; they went out to fight for something that needed to be done, in a territory that became an extension of the home domain in which they had complete control, where they were the managers.

The general picture, if you go back fifty, seventy-five, a hundred years in this country, was of the American woman as manager. She wasn't afraid to go anywhere alone. I think one of the reasons there's been so much commotion about rape recently is that American women have been accustomed to going wherever they liked. They'd wear long hatpins sometimes if they were going to a bad area. On the whole American women have thought that they could go anywhere and confront anybody, that they could walk right into a saloon and get that man and take him home and tell the barkeeper what they thought of him. They walk with a degree of assurance that has always astonished the rest of the world, especially those women who wear veils and who, when they have thought about taking the veils off, have hoped to become not like middle eastern men but like American women.

The division between the domain of women and the domain of men—and the willingness of the woman to take the man's place whenever it was necessary—is found over and over again. This did not make the woman into a soft, pliant, responsive creature who was interested in listening and catering to other people's moods. She managed the house and fed her husband and her children and the thrashers the way she might have managed a large cafeteria. You don't get the subservience of the traditional Japanese woman who burned the rice for one meal so she could eat burnt rice at the next. As long as the enterprises in this country were such that the woman in the home had a reasonably important domain, where she prepared the food, made some of the clothes, and made a great number of the decisions, demands for women's rights came from two groups. One consisted of women who had no relatives and no home. Very early, fathers and brothers and sons decided it wasn't their business to look after the spinsters in the family. They were all thrown into the labor market to support themselves. So defending those women who had to work and those who had no male relatives to support them was one part of the movement for women's rights. The other part was made up of women who wanted to get out there and fix things, who were concerned about peace, prohibition, antislavery, who wanted to take their ideas from the home out into the community. But they had enough to do and we didn't have a very seriously, nostalgically unemployed woman at home until the advent of the contemporary world of suburban living, in which we began confining women into homes in which they were not only just managers but managers who produced nothing. They simply manipulated gadgets. For the first time, really, in women's experience in this country the only thing a woman could say at the end of a week was, "Well, I got through the week and nothing happened." Now for a nice quiet little clinging vine to get through the week with nothing happening is fine, but for the average American woman to have nothing to say at the end of the week except "Nothing happened—the house didn't burn down, the children didn't break their legs, my husband didn't leave me, so it was a successful week" wasn't enough. And one of the things that we've been witnessing at present is that the feminist movement in this country is primarily a movement of women who were reduced to being nothing but consumers, making consumer choices and having no chance to be productive at all. The old picture of the woman who was as capable as a man—not as strong perhaps, and having other things to do besides bearing children, who could manage if her husband were away or if he died—has now spilled over to a very large number of women who are living alone and electing to live alone with their children.

A new book called *Hannah's Daughters*, by Dorothy Gallagher, is the story of six generations of strong American women, all of whom married men they shouldn't have and shed them. Today we think of such things as modern phenomena, but they aren't so modern; the woman who managed alone with her children is a very old phenomenon in this country. Now, however, we have nine million fatherless households, and we have many instances that are being heavily heralded by the media of women who have just gotten up and taken their children and left. These women have had extraordinarily little sense that they wanted to be part of an interlocking, cooperative household which they could manage. A household was quite a domain in the early days of this country, and women managed that domain very well. But today women don't have enough that is important to do at home.

We have turned the American home into a launching platform. In most countries, people retire into their homes to get away from other people, to be comfortable, to rest, and to be taken for granted. But the American home isn't a place where people are simply comforted and listened to and have their wounded egos patted. We push our children out as hard as we can: "Be independent, get out, leave, learn to stand on your own feet." Like the men and the children, women are also now launching themselves out from a home designed for people to leave.

Considering the implications of this general style of womanhood that's been built in this country, the present demand that women have a chance to participate in public life can be identified as coming just as much from the outside as it does from the inside. On the one hand, we've built a society that has a standard of living that forces married women to work, and on the other, women themselves demand the right to work. And we've moved into a position now where women are saying that if they're going to participate in public life, men have to participate in domestic life. This hasn't gone quite as far in this country as it has, for instance, in Sweden and in Cuba. But there's a continual demand now for the kind of legislation which permits women to operate as whole individuals—borrow money, buy property, do all the things that a man could do as a full, autonomous person—and a lot of pressure for changes in work regulations so that, for example, a man could stay at home and take care of his children when they're sick. But in this country, these moves are attempts to build a kind of equality of strength and equality of activity in which neither person is dependent—really dependent—on the other. That is, we have had as an ideal in this country the kind of individualism in which women as well as men—and children as well as adults—should be full, autonomous individuals, not dependent on anyone. We've carried this so far, of course, that it's very hard for us to really think in any kind of inter-dependent terms.

Everybody in this country who buys a house or buys some land and builds a house wants a view. Have you ever sat down and figured out what the world would be like if everybody had a view—which means that nobody would ever be where anybody else could see them? It never occurs to Americans that their house is somebody else's view, because everyone's aiming as hard as they can to find a place where there's nobody in their view. And this is another part of the same emphasis on completeness: independence of everybody else and, among other things, you'd like a view. American home-ownership is again a part of the same picture.

We're approaching a period in the world when what we're going to need to emphasize is interdependence—people's relationships to each other, the needs of children to be cared for by adults and also the needs of adults to be understood by children. We're going to be working toward an attempt at complementary types of relationships or shifting reciprocal relationships. So it is very important to look at this traditional American woman, and maybe for a moment, at the traditional American husband. American women right through time have dreamed about the sheik of Araby, but they never wanted to marry him. The sheik was a myth; they want to marry a nice, steady, good-humored, tolerant, good provider. That has been the ideal American husband. And his ideal is a woman who can stand on her own feet—can manage by herself if he dies; the degree of independence in each state for the husband and the wife is very strong.

We are trying to design a new kind of world in which there will be no activities which are distinctively male or distinctively female. This is something that we're moving toward at present, but there's no guarantee that we may not move away from it again. We have an original base in which American women, in a sense, are far less dependent and responsive than women in other societies and are accustomed to standing on their own feet, having their own checkbooks, and managing their own lives. If we want to create a general climate in which men and women are expected to do the same things interchangeably (drive taxicabs or look after the baby), we're going to have to consider the background of emphasis on autonomy, independence, and nonresponsiveness to other people. And we're likely to have a strong residue from these old attitudes. One of the things women do when they become independent is to stop breast-feeding, because breast-feeding is an exceedingly interdependent position. Bottles make it unnecessary for women to be tied to babies. Women don't carry babies anymore. They have baby carriages, or they strap babies in automobiles. When they're in a supermarket they put the babies in carts and push them around. At every point we've been denying any kind of dependency and we've produced, to some extent, alienated people who depend so little on other people because that's what's expected of them. And yet we're moving into a world in which we are going to have to know about relating to other people—people who need our strength and people who need our willingness to comply, to yield in many ways.

And so, one of the things worth thinking about is this relationship between the kind of woman we've been proud of and the kind of woman who's been proud of herself in this country. They are not the women of the period from the 1950's up to the beginnings of the women's liberation movement. Those women were a product of the modern suburbs—we didn't have them very long, and we won't have them again. I've been talking about the women from the beginning of our history to the present. We will want to think quite hard about whether we're going to continue this historic kind of style, in which everyone is looking for a place to stand on their own feet and no one is really willing to spend very much time conforming or complying or considering the needs of other people except as part of a kind of managerial complex.

Harlan Cleveland of the Aspen Institute for Humanistic Studies has in his career moved back and forth between public life and the groves of academe. He graduated from Princeton in 1938 and attended Oxford as a Rhodes scholar. His graduate work at Oxford interrupted by the war, he went to Washington to become an intern in the office of Senator Robert LaFollette, Jr., of Wisconsin. In 1944, at age 26, he was assigned to manage the economic programs of the Allied Control Commission in Italy. After the war he remained in Rome with the United Nations Relief and Rehabilitation Administration until 1947, when he was transferred to Shanghai to be director of UNRRA's China Program. He returned to Washington in 1948, where Paul Hoffman, then administrator of the Economic Cooperation Administration, assigned him to build economic aid programs in six other countries of East Asia. It was during this period that he used the phrase "Revolution of Rising Expectations" in the title of a speech. The term is attributed to him in Bartlett's Familiar Quotations. *He left Washington in 1953 to become executive editor, and later also publisher, of* The Reporter *magazine. In 1956 he became dean of the Maxwell Graduate School of Citizenship and Public Affairs at Syracuse University.*

In 1961 President Kennedy appointed him assistant secretary of state for international organization affairs, in which position he served until 1965, when President Johnson assigned him to Paris as ambassador to NATO and representative on the North Atlantic Council. It was at that time that he commented that he had the best post in the State Department: it was 3,000 miles from Washington and 10,000 miles from Vietnam. He became president of the University of Hawaii in 1969 and during his five years in that office succeeded in expanding and rationalizing the fairly new state system of public higher education. In the fall of 1974 he became director of the Aspen Institute's Program in International Affairs, with headquarters in Princeton, New Jersey. He is the author of several books, among them The Obligations of Power (*1966*), NATO: The Transatlantic Bargain (*1970*), *and* The Future Executive (*1972*).

America's
Not-So-Manifest Destiny

HARLAN CLEVELAND

"What we miss just now," a European said early in 1976, "is the naiveté of American leadership."

Americans are not in a mood just now for either naiveté or leadership. We moved into our quadrennial political combat season with a sigh and a curled lip and a shake of the head. "The electorate seems apathetic to the point of sullenness," says a political columnist. "Four out of ten Americans think it doesn't matter who wins the elections," says a pollster. Even the candidates, upbeat by profession, had to acknowledge the mood. Can the federal government be made "decent" again? one of them asked. "The majority of the American people don't think so, but I think the answer is yes."[1]

The answer had better be yes. For the times call for great actions by a great power—and the other great powers are for one reason or another ungreat, or at least unavailable as a source of fresh ideas or new institutions.

Our psychic disorder is more than ennui, yet not an acute illness. The polls show that most Americans think they and their families are doing all right; it is their leaders or their institutions that are not measuring up. We are going through a national change of life, and it makes us uncharacteristically nervous.

"The country's like a horse galloping along without a rider," says a black city councilman in Birmingham to a Scripps-Howard reporter in January of

1976.² A banker in Nashville, too, blames his jangled nerves on the government: "About all Washington needs to straighten it out is maybe the second coming of Christ." A veteran of Guadalcanal, a civil servant in Fairborn, Ohio, caught the spirit of our malaise: "We're good people, but you know America, they've got to blow us out of the water to wake us up to things." An entertainer in Nashville is not trying to be entertaining when he warns, "We'd better watch out or we're going to slide like those dudes in Rome did." He may not even have known that the 200th birthday of the American Revolution also marks the sesquimillenium of the fall of the Roman Empire in 476 A.D.

If anyone from abroad were writing about us today as perceptively as Alexis de Tocqueville did 150 years ago, he would surely be struck by the degree to which Americans have lost a shared sense of manifest destiny. Until about 13 years ago—I would date it from the assassination of John Kennedy, but each to his own historical taste—you could have asked the "average American" what kind of country America was supposed to be and what we thought the United States should be doing in the rest of the world and received a more or less coherent reply: The United States was opening up a frontier, building a citadel of freedom, saving the Union, binding up the nation's wounds, opening doors to business enterprise, applying science to work agricultural miracles, promoting universal education, protecting the right of workers to organize, unleashing the imagination of scientists and engineers, controlling the business cycle, getting rid of race discrimination, helping the poor and the very young and the handicapped and the disadvantaged, developing the world's first successful multicultural society. And as we looked abroad, we saw ourselves as fashioning a democracy others could copy to their benefit, an economic system that could make others rich (and, not incidentally, get them off our back), and a military power able, when sufficiently provoked, to frustrate the ambitions of dictators who thought they should call the tune in what we thought should be a world of diversity, peaceful change, and individual opportunity. We had declared our independence and made it stick.

Some of our shared ambitions, viewed through the prism of hindsight, are not nearly as attractive as they evidently seemed at the time. The shunting aside of the aboriginal Americans, the bitterness of the Civil War, the social consequences of hell-for-leather capitalism, the environmental fallout of enterprise, the long, unfinished story of racial discrimination, and the neglect of poverty were also part of the lusty economic expansion that was 19th-century America. The human cost of the American experiment came high.

In the crusading zeal of our international outreach, the arrogance of power also showed through. On Labor Day of 1901 Theodore Roosevelt, who was to become President only days later, told a crowd at the Minnesota State

Fair that our "world duties" included promoting "the civilization of man-kind," which required the United States to "put down lawlessness and anarchy in the Philippines." In making the Filipinos "a law-abiding, industrious, educated, and we hope ultimately a self-governing people," the Vice President proclaimed, "we are but carrying out the true principles of our democracy." [3]

Yet our double sense of mission was clear enough. It comprehended both the assumption that our own democratic experiment was (or at least was destined to become) a model for others to admire and emulate—as early as 1630, John Winthrop was saying that the colony of Massachusetts would be "as a city upon a hill, the eyes of all people are upon us"—and the notion that our probity and prosperity carried with them global obligations. One wartime President called on us to make the world safe for democracy. Another wartime President joined in an undertaking to "afford assurance that all men in all the lands may live out their lives in freedom from fear and want." And the spirit was still there in the now embarrassing hyperbole of the 1961 inaugural: "Let every nation know, whether it wishes us well or ill, that we shall pay any price, bear any burden, meet any hardship, support any friend, oppose any foe to assure the survival and the success of liberty."

But then—a trio of political killings, a debilitating defeat at arms (that is, at the arms we could bring ourselves to use), the upwelling of racial bitterness, the outbreak of campus disorder, the shock of insolent dishonesty in the White House, the loss of the dollar's value, the sudden awareness of dirt and damage and danger in the environment, the fear-inducing forecasts by computerized Cassandras, the rude awakening to energy interdependence, the advertised abuses of secret agencies, the unprecendented criticism from foreign friends, the disappointments with foreign aid, the revelations about corporate bribery, the embarrassing votes in the United Nations—that beacon of republican democracy which was supposed to help secure the blessings of liberty for "all Men" was flickering. The values we were trying to export even seemed to be under siege at home. If you now ask the first five Americans you meet what it means to be an American and what the United States means to do in the world at large, you are likely, even in this Bicentennial year, to get not a quotation from the Declaration of Independence but an expressive shrug and a puzzled frown.

The shrug is ambivalent, because the American-on-the-street is surrounded by evidence that U.S. institutions are durable and that his or her opinions can be influential. Racial contention and campus crises did not spill over into civil strife because American institutions on the whole adjusted to the demands for more fairness while resisting violence as the vehicle for moving toward it. Built-in checks and balances, featuring investigative journalists, courageous judges, and an aroused House of Representatives, did put an end to a President's corruptive reach for power.

Nor has the lesson been lost on our friends abroad. I have just been lecturing in New Zealand. Before, not after, one of my lectures a student leader in the audience made the most upbeat remark I have heard this Bicentennial year. "You know," he said as he greeted me, "whatever you as an American say to us tonight will be much more credible now, after Watergate."

Indeed if you look at the United States from abroad, as I have been doing for the past seven weeks—from Africa, from Europe, from New Zealand and Australia, from Japan—you are struck by the number of people who are waiting for the Americans to get up off the floor, recover some of that sense of destiny, and help get the world moving again toward a durable peace.

I will argue that the key factor in world affairs during the next few years is not the succession to Mao in China, not the outcome of the Lockheed scandal in Japan, not the food production statistics in South Asia, not the settlement (or renewal) of the Middle East war, not the price of oil or the size of automobiles, not the decision on how to deal with communists in NATO governments, not the transfer of authority from white to black in southern Africa, not the carousel of military governments in Latin America, not even the size and shape of the Soviet strategic arsenal. The key factor in world affairs these next few years will be whether, how, and for what purposes the American people decide to get back into the business of world leadership—in the service of new global tasks and with a style very different from those of yesteryear.

Just beyond the slough of our despond there is a mountain of essential and exhilarating work to be done, the kind of work that Americans, because of who we are and where we come from, are admirably equipped to tackle. It is no less than to help create a workable order in a world with nobody in charge, an enterprise which Americans with their pluralistic tradition should relish if anyone does. To be present at its creation may be a practical antidote to this mood of deep pessimism, this guilty self-denigration, this quite un-American no-can-do-ism that pervades the discussion of our destiny these days.

The tasks just ahead fall naturally into four kinds of attitude-changing and institution-building. They all reflect not our independence but our interdependence, because they all have to be tackled in league with other nations and thus blur the traditionally sharp line between "domestic policy" and "foreign policy." These tasks are:

- ⌒ to reconcile free institutions with full employment and fuller lives
- ⌒ to deal fairly with the global fairness revolution
- ⌒ to organize as global action the emerging ethic of environmental prudence
- ⌒ and meanwhile, to keep the peace.

The industrial democracies are caught up in a common crisis which each is treating as if it were uniquely national. The crisis is the agony of their success in maximizing choice for individuals and in producing enough to put a practical floor under the welfare of all their citizens. Yet more and more people in the "economically advanced" countries—in Western Europe, North America, Japan, Australia and New Zealand—are disemployed by modern urban and industrial systems and disaffected by the waste, the pollution, the crime, and the ugliness they produce along with rising indices of production. Cultural protest, experiments with new life-styles, an environmental movement, a yearning for lost quality, a resentment of squeezed incomes and obsolescent jobs, and a distrust of established institutions are everywhere the acolytes to affluence.

A lapel button distributed among educators by Alvin Eurich is devastatingly succinct: "Technology is the answer," it says, "but what was the question?"

The spread of education brings into the social process and political decision making whole new classes and categories of people, in larger numbers than can be readily absorbed and with have-not ideologies that cannot be readily accommodated.

National economic systems and the world economy seem to be working in ways that undermine some of the basic tenets of both market and Marxist theory. A "capital shortage" is a prime topic of conversation among capitalists. A century of American farm legislation aimed at preventing food surpluses is thrown into question as North America becomes the central granary of a world food system. Collectivization of agriculture and a dogmatic priority to heavy industry seem to keep Soviet food supplies on the ragged edge of disaster. And above all, the comforting doctrine that inflation and recession occur at opposite ends of the business cycle—a notion that seemed self-evident when I was studying Keynesian economics with a young Oxford don named Harold Wilson in 1938—has turned out to be unhelpful in dealing with the stagflation of the 1970's.

The pendulum of democratic governance swings between permitting too much joblessness and providing too much welfare. For a while, at prosperity's peak, we had a whole generation growing up which knew at age 20 that it would be able to make a decent living for life and started asking the questions only rich men's children used to ask, questions which adult society as a whole had not thought very hard about: If making a living is not going to be that much of a struggle, what are we going to do for adventure? If quantitative growth is too easy a goal, hadn't we better focus on the quality of life? Resentment of these questions and the absence of institutions in which they were the right questions to ask widened the generation gap and heated up the climate for campus disruptions and urban disorder.

When growth stopped and recession came—America again leading the parade—the "after affluence, what?" question was put in the freezer along with the campus disruptions, its place taken by the growing scandal of unemployment. That a great nation with strong trade unions and advanced industrial technologies could so mismanage its affairs as to dispense with the services of one-fifteenth of its people who want to work seems more and more puzzling to more and more people. Some of them are willing to trade in traditional freedom of choice for a new certainty of belonging—as totalitarian leaders ask, or force, their people to do. But most of us keep on feeling there has to be some way to make free institutions work to enable every citizen to earn his or her own social and economic relevance and enable each family to make and maintain a decent living. America, we believe, should be a place, as a high school student in Hawaii put it, "where everybody is a part of something."

To judge from the rhetoric this year, many Americans and most political leaders think this is essentially an American problem. But inflation and unemployment are a global epidemic, causing cabinet crises in a dozen industrial democracies and threatening democracy itself in several of them. A new creative spate of post-Keynesian theorizing and a new spirit of mutual assistance among the industrial democracies to make industrial democracy work better are urgent requirements of our time.

The crisis of industrial democracy coincides in chronology with the global fairness revolution—the demand of the newly articulate developing nations, calling themselves the "trade union of the poor nations," that the rich should help them more to develop faster and admit them sooner to the exclusive clubs where decisions are made about the world economy. International law based on freedom for all is shredded by nonobservance because it is seen as helping only those with the technological capacity to exploit it. Freedom from colonial shackles is revealed, in Werner Levi's phrase, as another name for neglect by those who have most of the marbles and still control the rules of the game.

The hell that has been raised by the "poor nations" has been loud enough and strongly enough pressed to produce a crisis in the international system—and some desultory negotiations have even begun in Paris, Rome, New York, Nairobi, and elsewhere. But the precondition for constructive bargaining is "a shared sense that bargains can be struck which advance the interests of all, that a political consensus can be formed by widespread realization that peoples of every race and nation are in dangerous passage together in a world of finite resources, ultimate weapons and unmet requirements." [4]

America's intellectual and political struggle to invent a diplomacy for planetary bargaining has been right out in the open for the world to watch—even though it has been overshadowed during the 1970's by a constitutional crisis and several investigatory spectaculars.

Beginning not long after he became Secretary of State by title as well as function, Henry Kissinger began to grapple in public with the implications of interdependence. Between November 1974 and March 1976, in a remarkable series of speeches in Rome (on food), Chicago (on energy), Paris (on international cooperation), Kansas City (on commodity agreements), Milwaukee (on the United Nations), Minneapolis (on moral foundations of foreign policy), San Francisco (on détente), Laramie, Wyoming (on interdependence), and Boston (retorting to his political critics), he outlined an approach to working with "a world of many centers of power, of persistent ideological differences clouded by nuclear peril and struggling for economic maturity and advance."

It was Dr. Kissinger's misfortune to be groping constructively toward a policy of pluralism in a leaderless world while the incumbent political leadership of the United States did not really know what he was talking about. With stalled negotiations on the Mideast and SALT, he was no longer being treated in Congress as a miracle worker whose new perceptions of a new kind of foreign policy rated leadership attention. He served an appointed President who saw his political nourishment (as several other aspirants for the presidency also did) in inward-looking nationalism and the fanning of popular resentments. He served in a cabinet with secretaries of defense, the treasury, and agriculture who presumably read his speeches but did not take them as policy guidelines.

Nevertheless, the State Department did succeed, with some help from an articulate minority of outsiders, in getting a presidential decision to announce at the United Nations on September 1, 1975, that the United States was ready for serious planetary bargaining. The announcement contained a laundry list of 41 specific proposals, most of them costless but all of them serious. The list, more than the rhetoric of reassurance, showed that the United States had come into negotiating range. In consequence, the United Nations' "Group of 77" reined in its radicals and welcomed the beginnings of bargaining.

Eight months later, the momentum of last summer has markedly slowed. One reason was the roiling up again of traditional UN polemics, highlighted by the anti-Zionism resolution and sharpened by Ambassador Daniel P. Moynihan's vivid defense of U.S. positions, which made him an instant folk hero in American public opinion and a symbol of American backlash in Europe and elsewhere. Another reason for the slowdown was that the rest of the U.S. government turned out not to be as ready for the beginning of bargaining as Secretary Kissinger had indicated. The imperatives of interdependence were not very much in evidence, for example, when an assistant secretary of the treasury announced that his department was not so sure the commodity agreements were in the U.S. interest, even though Secretary Kissinger has endorsed a "case-by-case" approach to their negotiation. The Department of Agriculture was equally dubious about the announced U.S. policy to create a world food reserve. And up on Capitol Hill both houses of Congress passed bills to create by unilateral action an American fishing zone out to 200 miles from U.S. coastlines—jumping the gun on the ocean law negotiations which were about to reopen in New York.

But apart from disinterest or disenchantment in the industrial democracies and a determination by both the Soviet Union and China to stick to offstage noise and avoid real contributions to a new economic order, there is a fundamental problem about this rich-poor relationship that must be frankly faced: It is the declaratory purpose of every human society to serve human needs. But most of the "poor nations" are not focusing on helping their own poorest citizens. The taxpayers in the rich countries have finally noticed this and begun to react.

Thirty years of development aid and technical assistance have been aimed at the supply side of the equation. The richer nations have spent millions increasing agricultural yields, training people to work with machines and manage large-scale systems, investing in the growth of all kinds of production. Judged by their own criteria these programs were successful—production and productivity usually rose. But looked at through the prism of basic human needs, a different picture emerges.

We succeeded in producing new strains of miracle rice without alleviating the old strains on the people who have to buy rice before they can eat it. We applauded when the per capita gross national product went up in this or that developing country and averted our eyes from the persistent, sometimes intensified, inequities inside these examples of economic "success." Leaving out China, where we do not really know the score, there are probably more poor people on earth—more malnourished human beings, more illiterates, more children without schooling, more families without shelter or access to medical care—than there were before "development economics" was invented. Something is wrong with the picture.

What is wrong is that too much of the effort, including too much of the international "aid" transferred, failed to trickle down to the people whose plight had made the political case for international aid irresistible. Part of the disenchantment with foreign aid in the United States is a feeling, often justifiable, that the help is not getting to the neediest people—that in the name of fairness an unfair result has been achieved. In 1975 a remarkable 91 percent of a sample of Americans (96 percent of those over 50 years old) agreed with the statement that "Too much of our foreign assistance is kept by the leaders of poor countries and does not get to the people." Yet when asked whether they would favor foreign aid if it got to the needy, an equally remarkable 79 percent said they would. And in early 1976, in spite of all, Americans asked about foreign aid were still lined up 52 percent for and only 18 percent against. Given the factual circumstances, it is a sign not of internationalism but of inattention for a reasonably well-informed American to be uncritically favorable to foreign aid and a sign not of isolationism but of mental health, to be asking, "Why should the poor in the rich countries help the rich in the poor countries?" [5]

There is of course a practical "poverty floor" in all industrialized countries and some developing ones, but a good many governments—including a few who raise the loudest voices in international debates about poverty—are not using what they have and what they can get from the international community to carry out what the World Bank calls "redistribution with growth" within their own jurisdictions. A group that met in Aspen last summer thought it saw a new moral imperative beginning to emerge in world politics: that each person on earth is entitled to a certain individual standard of living (*not* a per capita average) just by virtue of his membership in the human race. Such a "poverty floor" would vary greatly according to culture, climate, stages of life, working conditions, styles of living, and available resources but would certainly include a minimum intake of food measured in calories and nutrients, a development strategy designed to achieve shelter and sanitary conditions and health care sufficient to keep infant mortality down and life expectancy up to acceptable levels, and literacy training for all young people born into the society. Many other quantities and qualities go into making human settlements human. But without the physical minima, the deterioration of the body ensures degeneration of the mind and degradation of the spirit.

The limitation of population growth is critical. But the politics of planetary bargaining makes it better not to treat the control of population growth the way some Western analysts and political leaders would want it treated: as a goal in itself. Family planning is properly seen as an indispensable *means* to the goal of meeting minimum human needs, which can obviously be achieved sooner and more fully in societies where the rate of growth of population is not excessive—as planners in every rapidly developing country will candidly proclaim.

A couple of years ago, some international leaders were asking whether minimum human needs could be met worldwide without transgressing the "outer limits" of the biosphere. That question appears on preliminary analysis to be too easy:

On one important condition, we the people of the biosphere can probably lay our hands on more than enough of the relevant resources to enable all members of a growing world population to maintain minimum standards of life (some of them will even have a crack at liberty and happiness), without threatening the "outer limits" of an astonishingly rich and adaptable environment. If . . . .

The "if" is a question about our collective will to get on with it, our collective imagination to invent the institutions of fairness, our collective capacity to manage interdependence and finance great leaps forward. It would be foolish to treat this condition as anything but an enormous uncertainty. But it may help to know that the primary obstacle to making good on our 200-year-old pretensions about "all Men" may not be the resistance of nature after all, but merely the familiar and correctable orneriness of Man.[6]

To pump life back into a debilitated policy of "foreign aid" can have no attraction for an American political leader of whatever persuasion. But to help design a planetary bargaining process whose primary object is to meet minimum human needs is the kind of challenge that can reactivate two abiding traits of the American character—a deep humanitarian urge and a practical self-confidence in setting out to do what has never been done before.

The double crisis of managing affluence and meeting human needs also coincides with a new perception of global environmental limits. This is familiar ground to far less selective audiences than here assembled; the demands of environmental caution have even elbowed their way into prime-time television. Last year, for example, a brave and skillful TV writer managed to combine birth control and the ozone shield in a short episode of *All in the Family*. Mike didn't want to bring a baby into a world in which hair spray threatened to destroy the ozone and give everybody skin cancer. "All right," says Gloria at last, "Let's compromise. You let me have a baby and I'll let you have my hair spray. . . . Michael, you just can't go on being afraid of life."

In academic meetings, corporate board rooms, and government bureaus, the morose Michaels have mostly had the floor. But you will recall from your mythology that, while the doomsayer Cassandra was always right, the gods arranged for her to be always ineffective. Her modern disciples—the early Club of Rome for one—may have a more favorable record to show: they will be proved wrong, but partly because they *were* effective. In crying havoc they taught that our natural environment is finite and fragile. They were not very clear what to do about it; the prescription in that famous MIT study seemed to be some variant of "Don't just do something—stand there." Yet the lesson was taken to heart; environmental caution is already policy for dozens of governments and millions of individuals.

An emerging ethic of prudence suggests socially determined limits to the damage people should inflict upon their physical environment (air and water pollution, stripping of the land, thinning of the ozone shield); to the dangers inherent in people-managed processes (family planning decisions, nuclear power plants, chemical reactions, traffic accidents, weather modification, genetic engineering); to the rate at which people use up nonrenewable resources (fossil fuels, hard minerals); and to practices that affect the renewability of renewable resources (soil erosion, destruction of wildlife, overcropping of farmland, overcutting of forests, overfishing of lakes and oceans).

None of these limits is "there," set by Nature as a physical frontier. The popularity of projections about the biosphere's bounds has led to much loose thinking in which the "limits" are some kind of wall toward which we are rushing, with collision a simple calculus of rates of growth and elapsed time to impact. But in the case of minerals, for example, the "outer limits" of any resource are essentially determined by man's definition of the resource, man's perception of how much of it exists (only God knows for sure), man's decisions about how much he really needs, how much it is worthwhile for him to get at, how much he can reuse, and what other resources he can use instead.

Again there is a key question to ask about actions to reflect environmental prudence: Is the action international enough? We do not now have:

- an international system that negotiates and monitors agreed standards of air and water quality and reviews national actions that pollute beyond national frontiers
- an international system that keeps under review the damage and

potential damage from man-made processes and blows the whistle
on those that may affect people beyond national frontiers
 an international system that promotes exploration for and keeps a
world inventory of nonrenewable resources that may be needed by
people outside the nation where the resources happen to be found
 an international system that monitors world production of food and
fibers, maintains reserves of basic foodstuffs, promotes and assists
agricultural productivity, and provides for the exchange of timely
information on national harvests and food requirements.

These needed international systems will not be created without a good deal
of American push and American technology. Whether they can be created
even with our help will not be known until we try.

★ ★ ★

While we look for newly international ways to reconcile development with
democracy, human needs, and environmental prudence, the general peace
must also be pluralistically kept. Nuclear weapons made possible a new and
surprisingly durable form of general peace: a military stalemate with unusable
weapons. Would you have predicted in 1945 that by 1976 the third nuclear
device would not have been detonated in anger?

The stalemate works because the deterrence system is based on weapons so
powerful that even experts cannot show how they could be advantageously
used, so "hardened" that some could survive even all-out attack, and so
surrounded with safety devices that there has not been a disastrous accident
on either side in three decades of transporting, storing, and alerting them.

The peace we have kept is not the "collective security" of the UN Charter,
by which the good townspeople gang up on the dangerous outlaw and ride
him out of town. It is a new, technologically dynamic balance of power based
not on the certainty of response but on its uncertainty. The Soviets cannot
possibly know what we would do if they started using (as distinguished from
brandishing) their enormous nuclear arsenal; the reason they cannot know is
that we do not know ourselves. There is no "last war" from which military
planners can draw their inspiration and make their predictions. The "calculated risk" has become incalculable.

One effect of this deterrence by uncertainty is to render the largest weapons
the least usable—we put on in Vietnam a 10-year demonstration of their
unusability. But that very fact unleashes more smaller conflicts, of which

there have been some 40 during the period we still, curiously, call the "postwar era."

So the strategic stalemate is astonishingly stable. Almost equally stable is the standoff in Europe between NATO and the Warsaw Pact, and the world-wide naval confrontation is moving toward a dynamic equilibrium too.

We have been living for so long, almost comfortably, with these bilateral forms of stalemate that we have not given enough thought to the management of a multinational nuclear chessboard. In the past 20 years only one new nation per decade has tested a nuclear weapon. But since 1954 an average of one country a year has "gone nuclear" for the production of power. By the early 1980's there can be as many as 400 installed nuclear power reactors in 28 countries; the spent fuel rods from their operations would produce enough weapons-grade plutonium to make several thousand Hiroshima bombs a year.

As the politics of nonproliferation thus mutates toward a politics of pro-liferation, it is far from clear whether the multiplication of uncertainties will add to or subtract from the familiar bilateral stability. The existing nuclear powers have found nuclear weapons remarkably cost-*ine*ffective as instruments of strength in day-to-day diplomacy. But such weapons have not been tried as instruments of weakness; an Archbishop Makarios or a General Idi Amin or an Ian Smith or a guerrilla band with a nuclear device to brandish could in-troduce a very new dimension in brinkmanship. Public testing of weapons has certainly earned some political clout for China, for France, and maybe for India. Even without an observable test, the known potential to "go nuclear" is part of Israel's arsenal of deterrence. Brazil arranged to buy from the Federal Republic of Germany nuclear enrichment technology and re-processing equipment—the bridge from nuclear energy for power to nuclear energy for weapons—and shortly thereafter the American secretary of state visited Brazil to arrange for regular political talks to parallel the practice of consultation with European allies and Japan. Other nations that are thinking of "going nuclear" are not likely to believe that this was a coincidence.

In sum: Uncertainty demonstrably works as a deterrent when there are only two super scorpions in the bottle. No one knows how a growing crowd of smaller scorpions would act.

The increasingly heavy traffic in "conventional" arms may prove to be the most destabilizing element of all in the new polycentric balance of military power. The orders placed for nonnuclear weapons—no longer just the castoff or obsolescent matériel of the major powers but now including some of the most advanced technology—amounted to more than $20 billion last year. The United States, its government and its industry, accounts for well over half of this traffic, treating it as a good way to bring U.S. overseas payments into balance. Munitions makers, some of them semisocialized with heavy government investment, have regarded overseas arms sales as so important to their profit margins as to justify large bribes to intermediaries and government officials in the purchasing countries. Yet the net effect of permitting sophisticated weaponry to be sold to ambitious and in some cases precariously supported political leaders must be to help these leaders rule without consent, throw their weight around in their regions, and risk involving the nuclear-weapons states in regional quarrels that get out of hand.

In this case there is something the United States can do by unilateral action. Conventional arms control would have to start with a review by the United States of its role as chief pusher of addictive commodities. Since the sale of a modern weapons system gets us committed for the long term (for spare parts and follow-on systems), judgments about the sale of arms should be regarded as high policy. The range of our arms sales should not exceed the breadth and depth of our alliance commitments and security interests. Beyond that line, there are less dangerous ways than military merchandising to improve our balance of payments.

The argument for laissez-faire is usually that if we do not sell the weapons, others will. But the United States, as Dean Rusk used to say, is the fat boy in the canoe. Others are unlikely to mount an arms-sales program on anything like the same scale as ours. Besides, some of the "others" are Atlantic allies too. We do not know what could be accomplished by seeking restraints on the arms trade within the alliance because we have not seriously tried it. The nuclear suppliers, including the Soviet Union, got together last year and surprised themselves by coming out with a first agreement in restraint of that dangerous trade. Maybe it is time for the conventional arms exporters to have an equally well-publicized secret meeting.

In this context "arms control" is not something outside of or antithetical to "national defense." It is not enough to attach an "arms control impact statement" as an afterthought to each proposal for each new weapons system. If the first problem of peace is to keep military stalemates stale, "arms control" is not a specialized task for a fringe agency of government but is properly the centerpiece of the U.S. defense posture for 1977 and beyond.

Taken together—and we do have to take them all together—these four Herculean labors add up to the 20th century's third try at world order, the League of Nations having failed and the United Nations being unable in its present condition to cope.

The requirement is for a great creative surge of pluralistic institution-building in a world where no nation or alliance can call the new tune or write the new rules. And much of the world, in fear or in hope, is waiting to see what the United States of America is going to do about it.

The third try will have to include a system for relating international co-operation to minimum human needs; an international review of national decisions about growth, waste, and affluence; a complex of environmental-protection systems; a peacekeeping and peacemaking system, including arms control agreements and their enforcement; new systems for international cooperation on food stocks, energy supplies, transnational enterprise, shifts in industrial geography, development financing, and decisions about the money supply; and global systems for inherently global functions such as weather modification, broadcasting from satellites, ocean resource management, remote sensing technology, and research on even wider threats to mankind—damage to the ozone layer and the probability of extraterrestrial intelligence.

Merely to list such functions implies that these enormous tasks must all be undertaken by large international bureaucracies. My own preference—and my assumption, too—is the reverse: whatever can be done by local governments, private or mixed enterprise, voluntary nongovernmental organizations, and national governments should certainly not be done by intergovernmental bureaucracies and global assemblies. Small is not necessarily beautiful; the scale of human effort must match the size of the physical and social problems to be tackled. But even where the problem is inherently global, as the weather is, most of the operational components of a worldwide system can be national or subnational—in the World Weather Watch, most of the investment is Russian or American. Nor does every nation have to be involved in every function. In many cases regional groupings or consortia of those who want to cooperate in a particular activity (Intelsat, for example) may be the most practical approach.

Some functions may require at the international level only an agreement on rules of the game, with an occasional meeting to review them—certain trade agreements are examples. Others may require regular and intensive consultation, assisted by a secretariat—the allocation of radio frequencies is in this category. Still other functions may require international executives— examples are IAEA's nuclear safeguards, the World Bank's lending program,

NATO's military planning setup, and many other existing organizations. Where the operational function must itself be international, there may be a larger role for a political-rank collective executive (the European Commission model), to which nations can "lend" their sovereignty in situations where it cannot be separately exercised without leading to unacceptable levels of conflict.

So many functions, so many organizations, so many interlocking directorates, so much overlapping membership—but would we want it otherwise? We are seeking, not just settling for, a pluralistic world. The alternative is for some nation or bloc or ideological party to be in general charge, but we have already decided we do not want that and have fought three hot wars and one cold war to "make the world safe for diversity." A horizontal multiplicity of separate international systems, pulled together not by executive fiat but by the shared sense of need to work together to avoid the scourge of war, is more likely than some giant vertical pyramid of world governance to enable each people to develop in its chosen way with a maximum of international cooperation and a minimum of international dictation.

The style appropriate to the exercise of leadership in such an environment is plainly different from the aggressive dirigisme of colonial, military, and business leadership in earlier times. Consultation, openness, suasion, and consensus are the essence of horizontal leadership—in small communities as well as in the world community. But such a style should not be uncongenial to Americans who, together with their ancestors, have spent 200 years experimenting with the management of a society where no one is in charge, where separation-of-powers and checks-and-balances are supposed to keep anyone from making too much yardage at the expense of everyone else, where competition is a means of cooperation, and where we continue to think it possible to get everybody in on the act and still get some action.

The key to such a system is that rights are paired with responsibilities, that there are no free lunches or costless benefits, that each participant is responsible for the consequences of his participation. It goes better in French: Il faut vouloir les conséquences de ce qu'on veut.

In such a complexity, how can each participant judge his best interest and arrive mindfully at an acceptable action in common with others?

One way is to avoid ideology. If there is one clear lesson from the story of human cooperation in social enterprises, it is that people can agree with each other on what to do next if they carefully avoid agreeing on why they are cooperating. (Israel and its Arab neighbors recently agreed to help clean up the Mediterranean Sea together, in an arrangement negotiated by the United Nations Environmental Programme, without raising any of the contentious issues that have led to three wars between them in the past generation.)

As we approach planetary bargaining in these terms, we are hampered by a human propensity to mistake current trends for long-range destiny. The projection of population, the imminence of starvation, the profligacy of affluence, the fouling of air and water, the danger of accidents, the waste of minerals, the damage to soils, and the proliferation of plutonium can be readily spliced together to make the case for catastrophe. But the global predicament was made by human beings, and that has to mean that human beings can design their way out of it.

Will the mood of the American people permit any U.S. government to place a high priority on its participation in the third try at world order? The answer is not predictable from the available evidence. Some analysts of U.S. opinion have been impressed by statistical findings of popular indifference to international affairs, reading them as a return to isolationism. But the numbers can be read two ways.

In 1964, a sample of Americans were asked to name their chief worries; the top five items all related to international affairs or defense. A similar sample in 1974 named 16 domestic worries before mentioning the first international-affairs concern: keeping military forces strong.[7] In September 1974 Gallup found that 52 percent of Americans under 30 thought too much money was being spent on defense. Do numbers like these mean Americans have reverted to isolationism? It is equally arguable that it was quite perceptive of the American man-on-the-street to judge in 1964, shortly after the Cuban missile crisis but in the midst of a prosperity boom, that the chief threats to American welfare and well-being came from abroad—and to judge in 1974 that, with the Vietnam war being liquidated and talks in full swing on strategic arms limitation and mutual force reduction in Europe, the primary concern of a practical American should properly be inflation-cum-recession, a national energy policy, environmental issues, the dangers of nuclear power plants, racial discrimination in housing and the schools, corruption in politics, and crime in the streets.

Indeed, there is persuasive evidence that the American people have "gotten the word" on their interdependence but are waiting for someone to suggest what they should be doing about it. The National Commission on Coping with

Interdependence, chaired by Robert O. Anderson, spent the year 1975 inquiring into public attitudes. One report to the commissioners found that:

> by and large, people seem to be more willing than their leaders give them credit for to face up to the adjustments which international interdependence may require of them. The revolution in attitudes about, for example, environment and population, seems to have come out of the grass roots rather than leadership. . . . The polls continue to suggest that people-in-general are readier for a national energy policy than are their political leaders.
>
> To the extent that interdependence may impose burdens that must be widely shared—as the Arab oil embargo and future energy shortages may yet do—we the people are ready to make major adjustments in our life styles and workways if (a) someone with credibility tells us that it is in the public interest and (b) the distribution of the burden is obviously fair.[8]

Our Atlantic and Pacific allies have for so long been acutely aware of their dependence on other people's materials, markets, and military strength that it may be hard for them to understand how very recently this has become a matter to which American citizens at large felt the need to give much attention. Our continental economy, global defense establishment, and cultural vigor have been such that interdependence, if it meant anything at all, seemed just a fancy description of a one-way relationship in which others depended on America for food, education, television programs, science and technology, computer hardware and software, military deterrence, and political leadership. The reality was more reciprocal than our attitudes toward it, but that only came home to the American people at large when they had to sit for hours in long lines at the corner filling station because of faraway actions by a few Arab leaders.

"Every 'domestic' decision (on soybeans, on environment, on monetary policy, or whatever) has international implications, and every 'foreign' development (the Middle East conflict, a Soviet crop failure, a production facility for nuclear fuel, or whatever) has a ripple effect in our national economy and in American politics," said one of the reports to the National Commission on Coping with Interdependence.[9] The adjustment we now face, said the commission in its final report (March 1976), "will be to blur, then erase, the psychic frontier between 'domestic affairs' and 'international affairs.' "[10]

If few Americans now deny the intimate interconnection between faraway causes and highly personal effects, most American leaders still doubt the willingness of Americans to adjust their personal habits for faraway reasons. We have in fact done so on a national scale only in wartime. We can tell that our willingness is in doubt because most American political leaders still calculate that we are not prepared to do what they say in speeches needs to be done. During the past two years both the President and the Congress have been unable, despite encouragement from the polls, to bring themselves to believe that their constituents are willing to alter practices and policies Americans have long regarded as essentially private, personal decisions—how much to buy, what to eat, how fast and far to drive, how many children to have, whether to pollute, what to produce and sell, how hard to work, what to aspire to.

Such understanding is partly a function of education—what we learn about interdependence in school and college, from the media, and from each other. It is also partly a function of leadership: Americans were vaguely aware in 1947 that things were dangerously awry in postwar Europe, but it took a stunning act of leadership, the Marshall Plan, to convert a vague awareness into a 1948 act of Congress designed to do something decisive about European recovery.

Twenty-nine years ago when the Marshall Plan was invented, the decisive actions required to meet international crises were mostly taken by a couple of dozen leaders in the White House, the State Department, and the Congress. But nowadays the chronic crisis of interdependence, of which the facets called energy and food are only the tip of the iceberg, requires action by dozens of government agencies, thousands of private institutions, and millions of householders and automobile owners.

The style of national governance required in these circumstances is more akin to wartime leadership, engaging the cooperation of whole populations to take "domestic" actions for international reasons without which the requisite international cooperation cannot be arranged by even the most skillful diplomats. Such leadership goes far beyond the capacity to guide legislation into law; it involves not only persuading whole populations that interdependence requires changes in attitudes, assumptions, lifestyles, and workways but also eliciting millions of willing actions, more or less voluntary, backed up by the market economy, social pressures, public shame, and—only at the margin—governmental power. The search for this leadership is one of the hidden issues in the U.S. presidential campaign of 1976.

If the prospects for mankind cannot be transformed merely by the acts and enactments of political leaders, literally millions of Americans, through their thousands of nongovernmental organizations, need to develop the personal sense of direction, the world outlook, the feeling of individual responsibility for the collective outcome, which only an established few, educated in elite colleges and the best universities, used to need. Can we do it?

Americans come from a pioneering tradition. We share the psyche of immigrants to a promised land, and we still, I believe, think of ourselves as mobile and adaptable, welcoming change and assuming that it will be progress. We are learning, says my colleague Thomas W. Wilson, to adjust to a new economics in which air and water are not free goods, energy is not cheap, the oceans are not limitless, more is not better, and growth is not forever. A new political maturity, says Stanley Hoffman, entails awareness that leadership does not mean control, that we may well set an example without serving as a universal model, and that mere power can make us simply the biggest fly on the flypaper.[11]

Is it unrealistic to suppose that millions of Americans can change their minds, in time, about the nature of their nation, the style of its leadership, the very purposes of their own life and work?

We can change our collective minds in a hurry, it seems, when we know we need to. Who would have thought in the 1950's that attitudes toward population growth would bring the United States below replacement fertility rates by the mid-seventies? Who would have predicted the charisma of the environmental movement? Who would have thought that a war could be stopped not by a military decision but by a growing conviction, starting at the grassroots, that it just did not any longer make sense?

Yet these rapid changes in personal philosophy and social action have come about in a decade or two, often under pressure from the young, without much help from our major public and private institutions—national or local governments, corporations, churches, schools, and colleges. How much faster could we adjust our thinking on fundamental issues with the help of leaders who did not wait for the parade to form before offering themselves as drum majors?

Everything is tight these days. Money is tight, budgets are stingy, the margin of nuclear error is narrow, detente is unrelaxed, our fears and fantasies make us uptight. But imagination does not have to be in short supply; it is still our primary resource, and it is not even subject to the law of conservation of energy. The task is to fashion a workable, because pluralistic, system of peaceful change. The question is whether the American people will relish a new role of "horizontal leadership" or, in President Johnson's phrase made famous on President Nixon's tapes, "hunker down" and let World Order No. 3 be built around them without their participation.

You will, by this time, be in no doubt about my own choice. The world is an alarming place these days. But one way to describe an optimist is an alarmist in action.

Notes

[1] The columnist quoted is Mary McGrory in the *New York Post*, February 8, 1976. The pollster, cited by the *Wall Street Journal*, is Patrick Cadell. The candidate is Gov. Jimmy Carter of Georgia, during the New Hampshire primary (Tom Wicker, "Mr. Carter's Formula," in the *New York Times*, January 23, 1976, p. 31).

[2] Don Tate, "Bumbling U.S. Without a Leader, Citizens Complain," *Rocky Mountain News*, December 16, 1975.

[3] Theodore Roosevelt, "National Duties," a speech delivered at the Minnesota State Fair, September 2, 1901, printed in a collection of Roosevelt's speeches entitled *The Strenuous Life* (New York: P. Collier & Sons, 1901), pp. 228–42.

[4] *The Planetary Bargain: Proposals for a New International Economic Order to Meet Human Needs*. A Policy Paper of the Aspen Institute for Humanistic Studies, Program in International Affairs (Princeton, N.J., 1975).

[5] Miriam Camps, *The Management of Interdependence* (New York: Council on Foreign Relations, 1974). A similar formulation, that of Richard N. Gardner, found its way into Governor Carter's first major foreign policy speech of the 1976 presidential campaign (to the Chicago Council on Foreign Relations): "The time has come to stop taxing poor people in rich countries for the benefit of rich people in poor countries."

[6] Harlan Cleveland, "Introduction: The Fairness Revolution," in John and Magda Cordell McHale, *Human Requirements, Supply Levels, and Outer Bounds: A Framework for Thinking about the Planerary Bargain* (Princeton, N.J.: Aspen Institute for Humanistic Studies, Program in International Affairs, 1975), p. vi. Parts of the immediately following section are also adapted from this source.

[7] The useful statistical series on American concerns about international and domestic issues have been traced from year to year in the annual *State of the Nation* analyses, by William Watts and Lloyd Free, published by Potomac Associates in Washington, D.C. The relevant data are summarized in William Watts, " 'What Kind of People Are We?', " *Atlantic Community Quarterly* 13, no. 4 (Winter 1975–76), published by the Atlantic Council of the United States, Washington, D.C.

[8] "Foreword: The Most Important Subject," in Ward Morehouse, *A New Civic Literacy: American Education and Global Interdependence*, Interdependence Series, no. 3 (Princeton, N.J.: Aspen Institute for Humanistic Studies, Program in International Affairs, 1975, p. 5.

[9] "Foreword," in Adam Yarmolinsky, *Organizing for Interdependence: The Role of Government*, Interdependence Series, no. 5 (Princeton, N.J.: Aspen Institute for Humanistic Studies, Program in International Affairs, 1976), p. 3.

¹⁰ *Coping with Interdependence*, Final Report of the National Commission on Coping with Interdependence (Princeton, N.J.: Aspen Institute for Humanistic Studies, Program in International Affairs, 1976).

¹¹ Stanley Hoffmann, "Toward a Pluralistic World System," *Current* 175 (September 1975), pp. 48–52.

Library of Congress Publications
for the
Bicentennial of the American Revolution

The American Revolution: A Selected Reading List. 1968. 38 p. 80 cents. For sale by the Superintendent of Documents, U.S. Government Printing Office, Washington, D.C. 20402.

The American Revolution in Drawings and Prints; a Checklist of 1765–1790 Graphics in the Library of Congress. 1975. 127 p. $14.35. For sale by the Superintendent of Documents, U.S. Government Printing Office, Washington, D.C. 20402.

The Boston Massacre, 1770, engraved by Paul Revere. Facsim. $2. For sale by the Information and Media Services Office, Library of Congress, Washington, D.C. 20540.

Creating Independence, 1763–1789: Background Reading for Young People. A Selected Annotated Bibliography. 1972. 62 p. $1.15. For sale by the Superintendent of Documents, U.S. Government Printing Office, Washington, D.C. 20402.

A Decent Respect to the Opinions of Mankind; Congressional State Papers, 1774–1776. 1975. 154 p. $5.55. For sale by the Superintendent of Documents, U.S. Government Printing Office, Washington, D.C. 20402.

The Development of a Revolutionary Mentality. Papers presented at the first Library of Congress Symposium on the American Revolution. 1972. 158 p. $3.50. For sale by the Information and Media Services Office, Library of Congress, Washington, D.C. 20540.

English Defenders of American Freedoms, 1774–1778; Six Pamphlets Attacking British Policy. 1972. 231 p. $4.75. For sale by the Superintendent of Documents, U.S. Government Printing Office, Washington, D.C. 20402.

Fundamental Testaments of the American Revolution. Papers presented at the second Library of Congress Symposium on the American Revolution. 1973. 120 p. $3.50. For sale by the Information and Media Services Office, Library of Congress, Washington, D.C. 20540.

The Impact of the American Revolution Abroad. Papers presented at the fourth Library of Congress Symposium on the American Revolution. 1976. 171 p. $4.50. For sale by the Information and Media Services Office, Library of Congress, Washington, D.C. 20540.

The John Dunlap Broadside: The First Printing of the Declaration of Independence. 1976. 68 p. $15 casebound with slipcase, $7 paperbound. For sale by the Information and Media Services Office, Library of Congress, Washington, D.C. 20540.

Leadership in the American Revolution. Papers presented at the third Library of Congress Symposium on the American Revolution. 1974. 135 p. $4.50. For sale by the Information and Media Services Office, Library of Congress, Washington, D.C. 20540.

Manuscript Sources in the Library of Congress for Research on the American Revolution. 1975. 371 p. $8.70. For sale by the Superintendent of Documents, U.S. Government Printing Office, Washington, D.C. 20402.

Periodical Literature on the American Revolution: Historical Research and Changing Interpretations, 1895–1970. 1971. 93 p. $1.30. For sale by the Superintendent of Documents, U.S. Government Printing Office, Washington, D.C. 20402.

To Set a Country Free. An account derived from the exhibition in the Library of Congress commemorating the 200th anniversary of American independence. 1975. 75 p. $4.50. For sale by the Information and Media Services Office, Library of Congress, Washington, D.C. 20540.

Twelve Flags of the American Revolution. 1974. 13 p. $1.25. For sale by the Information and Media Services Office, Library of Congress, Washington, D.C. 20540.

Two Rebuses from the American Revolution. Facsim. $2.50. For sale by the Information and Media Services Office, Library of Congress, Washington, D.C. 20540.